Berlin

WORLD BIBLIOGRAPHICAL SERIES

General Editors:
Robert G. Neville (Executive Editor)
John J. Horton

Robert A. Myers   Ian Wallace
Hans H. Wellisch   Ralph Lee Woodward, Jr.

John J. Horton is Deputy Librarian of the University of Bradford and currently Chairman of its Academic Board of Studies in Social Sciences. He has maintained a longstanding interest in the discipline of area studies and its associated bibliographical problems, with special reference to European Studies. In particular he has published in the field of Icelandic and of Yugoslav studies, including the two relevant volumes in the World Bibliographical Series.

Robert A. Myers is Associate Professor of Anthropology in the Division of Social Sciences and Director of Study Abroad Programs at Alfred University, Alfred, New York. He has studied post-colonial island nations of the Caribbean and has spent two years in Nigeria on a Fulbright Lectureship. His interests include international public health, historical anthropology and developing societies. In addition to *Amerindians of the Lesser Antilles: a bibliography* (1981), *A Resource Guide to Dominica, 1493-1986* (1987) and numerous articles, he has compiled the World Bibliographical Series volumes on *Dominica* (1987), *Nigeria* (1989) and *Ghana* (1991).

Ian Wallace is Professor of German at the University of Bath. A graduate of Oxford in French and German, he also studied in Tübingen, Heidelberg and Lausanne before taking teaching posts at universities in the USA, Scotland and England. He specializes in contemporary German affairs, especially literature and culture, on which he has published numerous articles and books. In 1979 he founded the journal *GDR Monitor*, which he continues to edit under its new title *German Monitor*.

Hans H. Wellisch is Professor emeritus at the College of Library and Information Services, University of Maryland. He was President of the American Society of Indexers and was a member of the International Federation for Documentation. He is the author of numerous articles and several books on indexing and abstracting, and has published *The Conversion of Scripts, Indexing and Abstracting: an International Bibliography* and *Indexing from A to Z*. He also contributes frequently to *Journal of the American Society for Information Science, The Indexer* and other professional journals.

Ralph Lee Woodward, Jr. is Director of Graduate Studies at Tulane University, New Orleans, where he has been Professor of History since 1970. He is the author of *Central America, a Nation Divided*, 2nd ed. (1985), as well as several monographs and more than sixty scholarly articles on modern Latin America. He has also compiled volumes in the World Bibliographical Series on *Belize* (1980), *Nicaragua* (1983), and *El Salvador* (1988). Dr. Woodward edited the Central American section of the *Research Guide to Central America and the Caribbean* (1985) and is currently editor of the Central American history section of the *Handbook of Latin American Studies*.

VOLUME 155

Berlin

Ian Wallace

Compiler

CLIO PRESS

OXFORD, ENGLAND · SANTA BARBARA, CALIFORNIA
DENVER, COLORADO

British Library Cataloguing in Publication Data

Berlin. – (World bibliographical series; v.155)
I. Wallace, Ian   II. Series
016.943155

ISBN 1–85109–142–4

Clio Press Ltd.,
55 St. Thomas' Street,
Oxford OX1 1JG, England.

ABC-CLIO,
130 Cremona Drive,
Santa Barbara,
CA 93116, USA.

Designed by Bernard Crossland.
Typeset by Columns Design and Production Services Ltd, Reading, England.
Printed and bound in Great Britain by
Bookcraft (Bath) Ltd., Midsomer Norton

THE WORLD BIBLIOGRAPHICAL SERIES

This series, which is principally designed for the English speaker, will eventually cover every country (and many of the world's principal regions), each in a separate volume comprising annotated entries on works dealing with its history, geography, economy and politics; and with its people, their culture, customs, religion and social organization. Attention will also be paid to current living conditions – housing, education, newspapers, clothing, etc.– that are all too often ignored in standard bibliographies; and to those particular aspects relevant to individual countries. Each volume seeks to achieve, by use of careful selectivity and critical assessment of the literature, an expression of the country and an appreciation of its nature and national aspirations, to guide the reader towards an understanding of its importance. The keynote of the series is to provide, in a uniform format, an interpretation of each country that will express its culture, its place in the world, and the qualities and background that make it unique. The views expressed in individual volumes, however, are not necessarily those of the publisher.

VOLUMES IN THE SERIES

For Daniel

Contents

Contents

Introduction

Berlin is today the capital of a united Germany and, by virtue of that fact alone, one of the most important cities in the world. Unlike many other European capitals, it had not always seemed certain to achieve a position of such pre-eminence. Indeed, its history is characterized by 'a succession of false starts and abrupt endings' (Stephen Spender) and, as the following brief survey reveals, it is only over the last century or so that it has come to enjoy anything like the same status as, for example, London or Paris.

When the two halves of what was at that time still a divided Berlin decided to stage an impressive variety of cultural events to celebrate the 750th anniversary of the city's birth, they chose 1987 as the year in which to do so. Despite the fact that the Nazis had celebrated the 700th anniversary exactly fifty years earlier in 1937, the choice of date was essentially arbitrary, however, since the treaty of 1237 between Bishop Gernand of Brandenburg and the Margraves Johann I and Otto III mentions not Berlin but its twin settlement of Cölln.

It is not until 1244 that Berlin is mentioned by name in a document, and it is only in 1251 that it is first referred to as a town. By that time it was rapidly developing into a major trading centre in the Brandenburg region with a population of about 8,500. Its early economic significance is reflected in the fact that it had its own mint by 1288, the largest and most important in the region.

In the early years of the fourteenth century, however, Berlin's security was threatened by the general political and military instability which prevailed in Mark Brandenburg, the region of which it was a part. Because of his success in defeating the region's 'medieval gangsters' (Walter Kiavlehn) and thus bringing an end to the instability, a member of the Hohenzollern family was made Margrave of Brandenburg in 1415/17. Thus began five hundred years of Hohenzollern rule in the region, which came to an end only with the November revolution of 1918 and the abdication of Kaiser Wilhelm II.

Introduction

By the 1440s the Hohenzollerns had subjected Berlin to their rule, robbing the town of the autonomy it had previously enjoyed. Shortly thereafter it became the seat of the Hohenzollerns' power, accommodating both court and bureaucracy, but this was accompanied by a relative loss of political and economic significance until the beginning of the seventeenth century. The ravages of the Thirty Years War (1618-48) then left Berlin much weakened and with little prospect of a brighter future. It was the supreme achievement of *Kurfürst* (Elector) Friedrich Wilhelm to rescue and rebuild Berlin and Mark Brandenburg during a long period of rule (1640-88). He did so only after first disempowering the nobility, reducing the rights of the towns, setting up centralized administrative structures, and concentrating power in his own hands. He established a standing army to suppress opposition from without and within, turning Berlin into a garrison town in the process. Berlin rapidly overtook Frankfurt an der Oder as a major trading centre, partly by dint of welcoming Jewish and Huguenot immigrants who brought with them valuable skills. By 1688, the year of Friedrich Wilhelm's death, Berlin boasted 20,000 inhabitants – a modest number when compared to the 700,000 of Paris or London, but significant nevertheless, given the terrible damage inflicted by the Thirty Years War, and a solid basis for Berlin's future development.

In 1701, Friedrich Wilhelm's successor, the Elector Friedrich III, acquired the Prussian throne and henceforth called himself Friedrich I, King in Prussia. This was the somewhat inauspicious beginning of Prussia's gradual ascent to prominence among European states, with Berlin now laying claim to the status of a royal capital. Accomplished sculptors and architects, Andreas Schlüter among them, were entrusted with the task of giving the town a more gracious aspect. In 1694 the Academy of Arts was founded, followed six years later by the Society (later Academy) of Sciences, with Leibniz as its first President. In 1709 Friedrich amalgamated the five towns of Berlin, Cölln, Friedrichswerder, Dorotheenstadt, and Friedrichstadt to form a single, centralized community called Berlin.

By the time of Friedrich's death in 1713, therefore, Berlin boasted a wealth of fine new buildings and had taken on a much changed appearance. It had grown in size, and it had acquired a population of 60,000. Unfortunately, Friedrich had also left Prussia with an enormous burden of debts.

Friedrich's son and successor, Friedrich Wilhelm I of Prussia ('the soldier king'), represented a fundamental turning-point in the history of Berlin. Where his father had laid stress on the external trappings of power and had been prepared to spend large sums in the process, he set out to achieve military strength on the basis of prudent financial policies. The reductions in expenditure which he introduced led at first to severe economic hardship for many and to the departure from Berlin of almost 17,000 of its citizens within two years, although the population subsequently grew to about 90,000 as Friedrich Wilhelm's policy of encouraging new building enabled Berlin to more than double in area. It also became more and more of a military town, a reflection of the fact that the Prussian army under Friedrich Wilhelm increased in size from 40,000 to over 80,000 men. In the 1730s the king had a city wall built around Berlin. Six metres high and over fourteen kilometres long, it made military desertions more difficult and the collecting of taxes easier.

Although Friedrich Wilhelm did open two thousand new schools throughout Prussia and also encouraged the training of doctors, notably at Berlin's Charité hospital, he had little understanding of the arts and sciences. By contrast, Friedrich II ('Frederick the Great') encouraged Berlin's development into the centre of the Enlightenment in Prussia. Many of the leading intellectuals of the day, including Lessing, Nicolai, Moses Mendelssohn, and Voltaire, were part of the cultural blossoming ushered in by his reign. The face of Berlin was transformed by the building of the Opera, St. Hedwig's Cathedral, Prince Henry's Palace (later to become the main building of the University), a library (known today as the 'Kommode'), and a theatre, and by the development of both Unter den Linden as a major thoroughfare and of the Tiergarten park. In 1744 new life was also breathed into the Academy of Sciences.

Friedrich II was an ambitious politician, however, and led Prussia into a succession of wars, especially the Seven Years War (1756-63), which plunged Prussia and Berlin into an economic crisis from which they had to struggle hard to recover. Nevertheless, by the end of Friedrich's reign, Berlin's economy was again on a sound footing. The city had become the centre of the German textile industry and was the political, economic, and cultural capital of a Prussia which had been transformed into a major European power. With a population of 150,000 it followed only London (800,000) and Paris (700,000) among the major European cities.

Prussia declined after Friedrich's death, a process marked most dramatically by Napoleon's defeat of the Prussian armies at Jena and Auerstedt on 14 October 1806. Friedrich Wilhelm III and his wife Luise made their way to Königsberg, the garrison was withdrawn from Berlin since the city could no longer be effectively defended, and many of Berlin's well-to-do families took flight before the city was occupied by Napoleon's troops at the end of October.

The occupation lasted two years and cost Berlin dearly, but at least it allowed a group of reformers around Freiherr vom Stein to develop ideas for radical change which could be implemented once the French troops had left. Above all, reforms were introduced which, among other things, permitted Berlin and other cities a much greater degree of responsibility for their own affairs, provided for elections to Berlin's own city parliament, led to the founding of Berlin's own university (the Friedrich-Wilhelms-Universität, now called Humboldt-Universität) and other educational institutions, and brought about a reform of the army. When the Wars of Liberation broke out in 1813, Berlin became a focal point of the national resistance to Napoleon, over 6,000 of the 10,000 Prussian volunteers coming from the city.

In the three decades after the Wars of Liberation Berlin doubled its population to 400,000. Many of Berlin's new citizens came from other parts of Prussia, notably Potsdam. The modernization process which began with the onset of the Industrial Revolution in the 1830s brought with it the construction of a sophisticated railway system (the Berlin-Potsdam line opened in 1838) and led to the founding of new banks and other enterprises. Throughout this period, which was otherwise characterized by political conservatism and the suppression of any idea of liberal reform, Berlin witnessed a new cultural flowering. Its university enjoyed general esteem, boasting such eminent scholars as Fichte, Schleiermacher, Hegel, Niebuhr and Ranke. The Royal Academy of Sciences and the Academy of Arts acquired a European reputation. Karl Friedrich Schinkel conceived Berlin's most important new buildings, including the National Monument for the Wars of Liberation, the magnificent theatre situated on the Gendarmenmarkt, the (Old) Museum, the *Neue Wache* (New Guardhouse), Friedrichswerder Church, and the Schloßbrücke (Castle Bridge). The salons of Rahel Varnhagen and Henriette Herz, the circle associated with Bettina von Arnim, the literature of E. T. A. Hoffman, Heinrich Heine, and Adelbert von Chamisso, the music of Mendelssohn, Lortzing, and Meyerbeer – all combined to enhance Berlin's reputation as a cultural centre.

In 1848 Berlin became the focal point of the so-called March Revolution against political oppression, as a result of which the king, Friedrich Wilhelm IV, issued a conciliatory proclamation addressed 'To my dear Berliners'. He offered many political concessions to the rebels, but these may be seen as a ploy to achieve what the king called the 'taming of Berlin', and by November 1848 the old political order had been restored. Nevertheless, Berlin's reputation as a hotbed of dissidence was one which was never to desert it.

Berlin's expansion continued apace in the second half of the nineteenth century. Between 1857 and 1871 the population rose from 450,000 to over 800,000. By 1877 it had reached a million, and by

1905 it had risen to two million. Industrialization made rapid progress, the economy flourished, and by 1867/68 the city walls had been pulled down in order to allow the city to absorb Wedding, Moabit, Gesundbrunnen, and other outlying areas. But such rapid expansion had its cost. An acute housing shortage led to a rash of speculative building in order to meet the need for cheap accommodation for the city's many new and often poor inhabitants. The consequence of such unplanned building was the transformation of Berlin into what Werner Hegemann memorably called 'the biggest rent-barracks city in the world'.

In 1871 Berlin became the capital not only of Prussia but of the new German Reich achieved by the brilliance of Bismarck's political and military genius. The Reich's parliament now met in Berlin, but it was only in 1894 that it was able to move into its own building, the Reichstag, which even today forms such a distinctive feature of the city's landscape.

Berlin's new status and the enormous sums which France was required to pay as the price of its defeat in the Franco-Prussian War led to the economic boom years of 1871-73 (the so-called *Gründerjahre*). Even the crash of 1873 could not halt the continuous rise in the city's fortunes over the rest of the century. The electrical industry made spectacular progress, introducing Berlin's first electric street lighting in 1878 and its first telephone system in 1881. Between 1880 and 1886 the Kurfürstendamm was transformed into a splendid boulevard, fifty-four metres wide and over three kilometres long and leading from the heart of the city to the 'millionaires' suburb' of Grunewald. In 1879 the Royal College of Technology (today's University of Technology) was founded. Thanks to the enterprise of the publishing houses of Mosse, Ullstein, and Scherl, Berlin also became Germany's greatest newspaper city, and by 1930 it boasted no fewer than 149 daily newspapers.

Following the defeat of Germany in the First World War, the fall of the Hohenzollerns and the demise of Prussia, Berlin became the focus of political turmoil, including the November Revolution of 1918, the Spartacist rising of January 1919, the failed Kapp-Putsch by right-wingers who opposed the young democracy of the Weimar Republic (1920), and brutal assassinations such as that of Walter Rathenau, the Republic's Foreign Minister, in 1922. Nevertheless, Berlin's local government continued to function well, and in October 1920 Greater Berlin and its twenty constituent districts were created, bringing together under one administration the 3.8 million citizens who had previously been divided between Berlin (1.9 million), seven other towns (1.2 million), and many smaller communities. By 1930 the total had risen to 4.3 million. The Berlin of the 1920s was also the

Introduction

Berlin of Brecht, Reinhardt, Hindemith, Beckmann, Döblin, Tucholsky and the many other creative artists from all over Germany and the rest of the world who earned for this brilliant era the title of 'the golden twenties'.

How different were the 1930s, when Hitler's accession to power, the barbaric book-burning which took place on the square next to the Opera, the infamous *Gleichschaltung* (bringing into line) of all spheres of life including the arts, and the emigration of 'the greatest collection of transplanted intellect, talent, and scholarship the world has ever seen' (Peter Gay) brought the Berlin-centred cultural achievements of the Weimar Republic to an abrupt end. The Reichstag fire of 1933 and the Olympic Games of 1936 (during which Hitler notoriously refused to offer the usual congratulations to the most successful athlete at the games, the black American, Jesse Owens) are only two of the many inglorious events which stand out in Berlin's history during the period which immediately preceded the outbreak of the Second World War in 1939. Autumn 1943 saw the start of the bombing of the city, which continued with varying degrees of intensity until the last days of the War in 1945. It cost approximately 50,000 Berliners their lives and reduced almost thirty square kilometres of the city to ruins.

Germany's unconditional surrender was followed by the loss of twenty-four percent of the country's pre-war territory. What was left was then divided into four zones of occupation, each to be the responsibility of one of the victorious war allies. Although it was located well within the Soviet zone of Germany, Berlin too was divided into four sectors, one to each ally. This was in recognition of its special status as the capital of Germany since 1871.

Dissension between the Soviet Union and the other three allies meant that any hopes of achieving an early peace treaty which would settle the political arrangements for the shape of post-war Germany quickly had to be abandoned. The Soviets tried to compel the other allies to give up their part of Berlin by imposing a blockade. This lasted from 24 June 1948 until 12 May 1949 and was only lifted after the Western allies had organized an airlift of food and other essential materials which demonstrated their absolute determination not to give in to this pressure, whatever the cost.

The year 1948 also saw the founding in the Western part of the city of the Free University of Berlin. Its name reflects the reason for its existence: strong dissatisfaction with heavy-handed Communist interference in the running of the Humboldt University in the Eastern sector of the city and the determination to preserve academic freedom. Ironically, the important role played by the Americans in setting up the Free University did not prevent it from becoming in the 1960s a forum for the student protest movement which objected to the pervasive influence of 'the American way of life', the Vietnam War, government policies in West Germany, the country's failure to face up to its Nazi past, and the hierarchical structures of the traditional German university.

Since any decision about the post-war status of Berlin required the agreement of all the allies, the development of the Cold War meant that it was Bonn and not West Berlin which became the capital of the Federal Republic of Germany (FRG) when that country came into being in September 1949. However, this did not prevent the German Democratic Republic (GDR) from declaring that East Berlin was its capital.

Three important events stand out in the forty-four years of Berlin's division. On 17 June 1953 East Berlin building workers who were engaged on constructing the prestigious Stalin-Allee staged an uprising in protest against a deterioration in their working conditions. What had started as a local industrial dispute quickly spread to other parts of the country. It also turned into a political protest directed against the Communist régime. Although *agents provocateurs* from the West may have played a part in fomenting the unrest, there is little doubt that the uprising represented a severe blow to the prestige of a government which claimed to be the voice of the people. The FRG was not slow to derive what propoganda advantage it could from the incident, declaring the 17th of June an annual national holiday and renaming a major thoroughfare in West Berlin the Street of the 17th of June.

The construction of the Berlin Wall on 13 August 1961 represented a second defeat for the East German régime. Try as it did to argue that the Wall's purpose was to protect the country's burgeoning socialist system from attack by Western imperialists, few in the West were not convinced that the real reason was to staunch the alarming flow of its own citizens to the West, where they hoped to find better economic opportunities and political freedom. Forming a ring 166 kilometres long around West Berlin, of which forty-six kilometres defined the border between the two halves of the city, the Wall remained for twenty-eight years a particularly ugly symbol of the division of Berlin, Germany, and Europe. It exposed West Berlin to the very real danger of a slow, lingering death because of its exposed position as a small island surrounded by a Communist sea. That it survived is due in no small part to the determination of the three Western allies, the hardy resolve of the West Berliners themselves, and a remarkably high level of subsidy by the Federal German government. This included such measures as attractive tax incentives for investors in the city's industrial infrastructure, special monthly payments to the city's wage-earners, and steps to persuade young people to stay in or move to Berlin (including the exemption of young men from military service).

A third major event occurred when the erstwhile allies of the Second World War signed the Four Power Accord on Berlin (also known as the Berlin Accord) in September 1971. This was one of the principal successes of the policy of détente which had been developed by the United States and the Soviet Union during the late 1960s. Détente had provided the favourable climate which allowed the government of Willy Brandt to introduce and implement its so-called *Ostpolitik*, a more open and liberal policy towards contacts with Communist régimes in the Eastern bloc in general and in East Berlin in particular. By stipulating that negotiation and not force must be the method of dealing with any future disputes in Berlin, the Accord provided the essential framework of stability which made possible a succession of treaties and agreements between the FRG and the GDR, above all the Basic Treaty which was signed in December 1972.

Brandt, who had been Mayor of Berlin at the time the Wall was constructed, was convinced that only by normalizing relations with the East could an end be put to the process by which Germans on both sides of the Wall were being denied contact with each other and were therefore gradually but inexorably growing further and further apart. The Accord did much to make at least a degree of normalization possible. After years of being cut off from one another, Berliners in both halves of the city had many more opportunities to establish personal contact by letter and telephone. The number of visits by West Berliners and West Germans to East Berlin and the rest of the GDR jumped dramatically. Traffic in the opposite direction was on a more limited scale and largely restricted to the relatively free movement of pensioners, but the number of people allowed to travel West on urgent family matters did also increase noticeably. In addition, the Western media were able to operate with more freedom in the East, producing regular first-hand reports on life there and interviewing ordinary East Berliners and other citizens of the GDR whenever they saw an opportunity to do so.

Egon Bahr, Brandt's chief negotiator with the GDR, insisted that Berlin was the touchstone of détente. Despite some areas of sensitivity (for example, fundamental disagreement on the exact nature of the 'links' which both sides agreed did exist between West Berlin and the Federal Republic), the Accord proved an effective basis for the development of inter-governmental relations throughout the 1970s and 1980s. It also helped to produce an impression of stability and normality, however, which made any idea of German unification appear to most Berliners and Germans to be an illusion or at best a very distant possibility.

The sudden collapse of the Wall on 9 November 1989 therefore took Berlin and the world by surprise. The rapid progress towards unification which followed means that Berlin today finds itself at yet another turning-point in a history rich in such turning-points. It may no longer be the banking and commercial centre of Germany, but unification has clearly led to a rebirth of its ambition. After a passionate and at times acrimonious national debate the Federal Parliament voted on 20 June 1991 by a modest majority to make Berlin and not Bonn both capital and seat of government of a united Germany. The city is currently struggling with the task of planning and financing the kind of major developments which will be required if it is to meet the challenge of its new role. It aims to take full advantage of its geographical position at the centre of a united Europe to act as a meeting-point between East and West. Much energy is being invested in promoting and building on the city's reputation as a cultural metropolis. A bid is being prepared to host the Olympic games in the year 2000. Careful thought is being given to the possibility of uniting with the surrounding area of Brandenburg by the end of the century in order to form a single, strong *Land* which will represent a more significant presence in the German federal system. It is recognised that major investments in the city's infrastructure will be required if, as anticipated, the population rises to around six million in the foreseeable future.

All this is happening at a time of intense social pressures, of which an alarming rise in the crime rate and the insidious spread of violence against foreigners are only two obvious indications. Moreover, on 19 October 1992 a leading Berlin newspaper, the *Berliner Zeitung*, reported that a survey which it had commissioned had revealed that thirty-seven percent of all Berliners felt that their quality of life had deteriorated since unification, while forty-nine per cent believed the future would bring a (further) deterioration. Perhaps surprisingly, only one third of East Berliners felt the future would bring an improvement, while a quarter believed the situation would grow worse. On 11 January 1993 the same newspaper published the results of a further survey, which showed that, three years after the fall of the Berlin Wall, sixty-eight per cent of all Berliners still believed that their city was not truly unified.

Of particular concern is the evidence that Berlin's financial foundations are anything but secure. The enormously high level of investment required in the eastern half of the city is a particularly heavy drain on resources. The astronomical cost of the so-called 'transformation process' by which the territory of the former GDR is to be brought up to the standard of living enjoyed in the western parts of Germany also means that the Federal government is anxious to withdraw as soon as possible the high level of subsidy which West Berlin needed at the height of the Cold War and which (critics argue) a united Berlin no longer merits. The major challenge facing Berlin in the years ahead is how to balance financial prudence with the ambition of providing a united Germany with the dynamic, internationally-minded capital city it deserves.

The bibliography
The bibliography aims to provide the reader with a guide to published materials on Berlin. Given the wealth of such materials, it is necessarily selective in nature. Since it was written primarily with an English-speaking readership in mind, it gives preference to sources in English where these are available.
The volume also reflects to some degree my own interests and areas of expertise. Nevertheless, I have attempted to make the coverage of topics as comprehensive as possible despite the obvious limitations of space. The volume therefore follows the standard format of the World Bibliographical Series, organizing its 429 annotated entries under a number of topic headings which are common to all the volumes in the series and adding to that number only where necessary. In general, each numbered entry refers to one work only, but in some cases reference is made to one or more additional, related titles. All titles are also listed in the index.
A particular problem arose from the fact that an almost embarrassing richness of sources in some areas contrasted markedly with a relative dearth in others, making it difficult to achieve a selection which was both comprehensive in its scope and yet representative of this essential imbalance. I hope the reader will judge that I have been reasonably successful in this regard.

Acknowledgements
Much of the work on this bibliography would have been impossible without access to the resources of the British Library in London and the Library of Congress in Washington DC. I am grateful to the staff of both institutions for their invaluable help across a period of four years. I should also like to thank my colleagues in the Library at the University of Bath for their assistance in locating some materials which I would otherwise not have been able to consult. A final word of gratitude must go to Dr. Robert G. Neville for his invitation to make my second contribution to the World Bibliographical Series and for the unfailing good humour with which he has supported my work.

Ian Wallace
Bath
January 1993

Berlin and Its People

General

1   **Living in cities: five comparative and interdisciplinary case studies about living in inner cities.**
Edited by Habitat Forum Berlin.   Berlin: Metropol, 1990. 87p.
This collection of case studies compares five very different (inner) cities, including Berlin, whose history, architecture and city planning are considered. Numerous photographs, diagrams, and maps help to bring out the cultural, social and economic similarities and differences. Particular attention is paid to the different lifestyles found in these various inner cities. A volume which pursues a similar theme but which is designed primarily for readers aged between nine and thirteen is Barbara Einhorn's *Living in Berlin* (London, Sydney: Macdonald; Morristown, New Jersey: Silver Burdett, 1986. 45p.). This lucid and attractively-illustrated work provides a good introduction to life in East and West Berlin. The text provides a balanced impression of what life was like on both sides of the Wall in the 1980s, and the choice and layout of photographs is excellent. A map of the city and index are included. Another book which has the same title and which is also designed for children was published a few years earlier, i.e., Angelika Wagner, *Living in Berlin*. (Hove: Wayland, 1980. 2nd impression 1981. 52p. bibliog.) [Living in Famous Cities].

2   **Views of Berlin.**
Edited by Gerhard Kirchhoff.   Boston, Massachusetts; Basel, Berlin: Birkhäuser, 1989. 297p. bibliog.
Based on the proceedings of a symposium held in Boston, this volume assembles chapters by twenty-three distinguished contributors. These are divided into four sections dealing with Berlin as a political focus of East and West, the development of the city's distinctive culture, personal experiences of Berlin, and Berlin as a thriving city. The book is illustrated with numerous photographs and figures.

3   **Preußens Adoptivkinder.** (Prussia's adopted children.)
Horsta Krum, foreword by Bishop Martin Kruse.   Berlin (West): Arani,
1985. 222p.

Written by the pastor of the Französische Kirche in Berlin, this concise history of the
Huguenots' emigration from France to Prussia after the Revocation of the Edict of
Nantes by Louis XIV in 1685 is based on the nine volumes devoted to the subject
written by the historians Erman and Reclam between 1782 and 1789. This volume
contains numerous photographs and also includes engravings by Daniel Chodowiecki.
Three works which trace the history of the Huguenots in Berlin up to the present are
Herrmann Schreiber, *Auf den Spuren der Hugenotten*, Munich: List, 1983 (320p. 6
maps.); Rudolph von Thadden and Michelle Magdelaine, *Die Hugenotten 1685-1985*,
Munich: C. H. Beck, 1985 (243p.); and G. Bregulla and W. Gottschalk, *Die
Hugenotten in Berlin*, Berlin, (East): Union, 1987 (420p. 104 illustrations).

4   **Weißensee: ein Friedhof als Spiegelbild jüdischer Geschichte in Berlin.**
(Weißensee: a cemetery as a mirror of Jewish history in Berlin.)
Peter Melcher.   Berlin (West): Haude & Spener, 1987. 80p.

The Jewish cemetery in the Weißensee district of Berlin was opened in September
1880. Peter Melcher's fascinating booklet sees in the history of the cemetery a reliable
reflection of the history of the Jews in Berlin over the last century. The volume
includes numerous black-and-white photographs.

5   **The Berliners: portrait of a people and a city.**
Walter Henry Nelson.   New York: David McKay Company; London;
Harlow, England: Longmans, 1969. 434p. bibliog.

Based on interviews with over 1000 Berliners, this is a lively and very personal
assessment of Berlin and its citizens by a man who admits to ambivalent feelings
towards his subject. As a boy he had been forced to flee with his family from Berlin to
Vienna in 1940 (his father worked for the US Foreign Service), and in 1948 he found
himself back in the city as part of US Army Military Intelligence. The book also
contains a readable account of Berlin's history, while chapters 17 and 18 deal with
escapes and attempted escapes from East Berlin to the West.

Books of photographs

6   **Berlin: capital of the German Democratic Republic.**
Anonymous, translated from the German by Intertext.   Dresden, GDR:
Verlag Zeit im Bild, 1987. 88p.

This glossy paperback, produced as part of the celebrations to commemorate the 750th
birthday of Berlin, contains over 150 photographs (the vast majority in colour) as well
as a short, self-congratulatory text (p. 10-17) in which (East) Berlin is described as 'the
centre of a politically stable and economically efficient country'. Despite the hollow
laugh which such a claim now inevitably provokes, the book remains of interest as an
important example of the way in which the GDR sought to project a positive image of
its achievements to the outside world.

7 **Berlin um 1900.** (Berlin around 1900.)
Edited by Archiv für Kunst und Geschichte, foreword by Justus Göpel.
Munich: Hueber, 1986. 160p.

Herbert Kraft provides detailed commentaries on seventy superb photographs which Lucien Levy took of Berlin around the turn of the century. Little is known of this French photographer except that he made frequent expeditions to Berlin between 1890 and 1910 in order to make a series of splendidly evocative photographs of the city's streets, squares, parks, and monuments.

8 **Berlin! Berlin!**
Friedemann Bedürftig, foreword by Richard von Weizsäcker. Hamburg: Carlsen, 1991. 80p.

Published during the debate about whether Berlin or Bonn should be the seat of government in a united Germany, this volume clearly shows the author's support for Berlin. In his foreword the President of the Federal Republic reiterates his well-known support of the case for the city. Little wonder that Berlin's Senator for Urban Development and the Environment, Volker Hassemer, welcomed the appearance of the book both as an ideally-timed and 'helpful' contribution to the debate and as a fitting farewell to a city landscape which, he declared, would look very different in twenty years' time. The message of the volume's 125 photographs is reinforced by short accompanying texts in German. Perhaps inevitably in such a work, the city is seen only from its best side, with no reference to demonstrations, run-down areas, homelessness, or the drugs scene.

9 **Berlin East and West in pictures.**
David Binder, introduction by Charles B. Anderson. London; Melbourne, Australia; Johannesburg: Oak Tree Press, 1965, rev. ed. 64p.

First published shortly after the construction of the Berlin Wall, this book remains worth consulting today for its numerous photographs of Berlin in the late 1940s and the 1950s. The accompanying text is generally factual in nature, its anti-communist undertone being largely held in check. It is divided into six sections: the area; history; the Wall; the people; the economy; and the future.

10 **Berlin.**
Photographs by Stephane Duroy, text by Philippe Ganier Raymond.
London: Merehurst Press, 1986. 128p.

A warts-and-all, yet curiously poetic impression of Berlin is conveyed by the ninety or so colour photographs which are contained in this book. The accompanying text is in English.

11 **Berlin.**
Edited by Bernd Ehrig. Berlin (West): Ehrig, 1988. 156p.

Contains 125 photographic impressions of Berlin yesterday and today, of which forty-one are in colour. The accompanying text is in German, English, French, Spanish, and Italian.

3

Berlin and Its People. Books of photographs

12 **Berlin.**
Text by Michael Ellsäßer, photographs by Erhard Pansegrau, translated from the German by Lenore Lengefeld. Munich: Bruckmann, 1987. 100p. index. map.
Fifty-four colour photographs illustrate this introduction to Berlin, which provides a summary of the city's history, discusses the significance of the Wall, describes the sight on the Kurfürstendamm, and looks at the 'other world' in East Berlin. An English translation of the text is provided on p. 75-95.

13 **Die Mauer: Monument des Jahrhunderts/monument of the century.**
Text by Wolfgang Georg Fischer, photographs by Fritz von der Schulenburg, chronology by Hans-Jürgen Dyck, translated from the German by Martin Crellin, William C. Flowe, Philip N. Hewitt, Michael Robinson. Berlin: Ernst & Sohn, 1990. [n.p.].
This excellent collection of photographs of the Berlin Wall is accompanied by a fascinating text in German and English. A useful chronology of the Berlin Wall within the context of world history (1961-90) completes the volume.

14 **Berlin im Abriß: Beispiel Potsdamer Platz.** (Berlin in outline: the example of the Potsdamer Platz.)
Janos Frecot, Helmut Geisert, Hartmut Kurschat, Andreas Reidemeister, Goerd Peschken, Gary Rieveschl, Raffael Rheinsberg, Julius Kohte. Berlin (West): Berlinische Galerie, 1981. 268p. bibliog.
This catalogue for an exhibition, which showed the changing face of Berlin over the years as reflected by the Potsdamer Platz, contains an excellent selection of photographs with helpful commentaries. It also includes a list of houses of art-historical value in Berlin and its suburbs which was drawn up by Julius Kohte and first published in 1923. Many of the houses it names have since been lost to the War or the city planners.

15 **Berlin: frühe Photographien Berlin 1857-1913.** (Berlin: early photographs of Berlin 1857-1913.)
Janos Frecot, Helmut Geisert. Munich: Schirmer/Mosel, 1984. 220p. bibliog.
Presents 220 photographs of Berlin, all taken from the city's own various collections.

16 **Berlin between the wars.**
Thomas Friedrich, foreword by Stephen Spender, translated from the German by Stewart Spencer. New York: Vendome Press, 1991. 240p. bibliog.
This excellent volume assembles a fine collection of photographs, many of which are selected from extensive archives in Berlin. In combination with an excellent text, they paint a powerful portrait of Berlin between two World Wars. The British edition was published under the title *Berlin: a photographic portrait of the Weimar years 1918-1933* (London: Tauris Parke, 1991).

7   **Das große Berlin: Photographien 1899-1935.** (The great city of Berlin:
    photographs 1899-1935.)
    Edited by Wolfgang Gottschalk.   Berlin: Argon, 1991. 152p.
This excellent book contains photographs by Max Missmann (1874-1945) which
splendidly recreate the Berlin of the first third of the twentieth century. A companion
volume from the same publisher is devoted to Missman's evocative photographs of
Berlin's city squares: *Berliner Plätze. Photographien von Max Missmann*, edited and
with a commentary by Hans-Werner Klünner, afterword by Wolfgang Gottschalk
Berlin: Argon, 1992). A comprehensive collection of Missmann's work can be found
in the Märkisches Museum in Berlin.

8   **Berlin the capital: yesterday-today-tomorrow; 130 photographs.**
    Otto Hagemann, translated from the German by Patrick Lynch,
    introduction and notes to illustrations by Felix A. Dargel.   Berlin
    (West): Arani, 1956. 168p.
Contains 130 evocative, black-and-white photographs of Berlin as it was both before
and immediately after the Second World War.

9   **Berlins Stunde Null 1945.** (Berlin's zero hour 1945.)
    Rolf Italiaander, Arnold Bauer, Herbert Krafft.   Bindlach, Germany:
    Gondrom, 1990. 175p. bibliog. map.
This volume, a special edition of a book which first appeared in 1979 (Düsseldorf:
Droste), contains 170 black-and-white photographs which present a vivid impression of
life in Berlin at the end and in the immediate aftermath of the Second World War.
Making use of the diary which he kept in April and May 1945, Rolf Italiaander
provides a subjective account of the last days of the War from the perspective of one
inhabitant of Berlin. Arnold Bauer describes the re-awakening of cultural life in the
city, while Herbert Krafft discusses Berlin's parlous economic situation after the
cessation of hostilities.

20 **Das ist Berlin! Die deutsche Hauptstadt und ihre Geschichte.** (That's
    Berlin! The German capital and its history.)
    Winfried Maaß, with contributions by Laurenz Demps, Heinrich
    Jaenecke, Rolf Schneider, Wolf Jobst Siedler, Gerhard Zazworka.
    Hamburg: Gruner & Jahr, in co-operation with the Berliner Zeitung
    (Sternbuch), 1992. 160p.
An attractively produced pictorial history of Berlin. The contributors' essays as well as
the helpful commentaries on a fine collection of photographs are all translated into
English (by Dave Corbett and Chris Wright) in a twenty-page booklet which
accompanies the volume.

21 **Das Berliner Schloß.** (The Berlin Palace.)
    Goerd Peschken, Hans-Werner Klünner, with the assistance of Fritz-
    Eugen Keller, Thilo Eggeling.   Frankfurt am Main, Germany; Vienna,
    Berlin (West): Ullstein/Propyläen, 1982. 557p. bibliog.
The 439 photographs contained in this volume provide a splendid pictorial record of
the Berlin Palace which once stood in the heart of the city. It was bombed in the

5

Berlin and Its People. Books of photographs

Second World War but could undoubtedly have been restored to its former glory if the East German leader, Walter Ulbricht, had not chosen to regard it as an undesirable relic of Germany's past and therefore ordered its demolition. The photographs are accompanied by a detailed and readable account of the palace's history which stretche over five centuries.

22 **Berlin '90.**
Edited by Presse- und Informationsamt des Landes Berlin. Berlin: Presse- und Informationsamt, 1990. 80p. (Berliner Forum 1/90).

An attactive, pocket-sized volume of colour photographs with an accompanying text in German, English, French, and Spanish (English version by Brigitte Amedinck). Produced immediately after the fall of the Berlin Wall, it is available free of charge to visitors to Berlin from the Press and Information Office in Berlin.

23 **Heinrich Zille: Photographien Berlin 1890-1910.** (Heinrich Zille. photographs of Berlin 1890-1910.)
Winfried Ranke. Munich: Schirmer/Mosel, 1985. 2nd rev. ed. 280p. bibliog.

Contains the first attempt to present systematically a selection from Heinrich Zille's work as a photographer. In all, 199 photographs are reproduced, the result being a fascinating evocation of Berlin at the turn of the century.

24 **Ostberlin: die andere Seite einer Stadt.** (East Berlin: the other side of a city.)
Lutz Rathenow, photographs by Harald Hauswald, afterword by Jürgen Fuchs. Berlin: Basisdruck, 1990. 133p.

The first version of this book, containing 177 photographs by Harald Hauswald, appeared in 1987 under the title *Ostberlin. Die andere Seite einer Stadt in Texten und Bildern* (East Berlin. The other side of the city in texts and pictures. Munich, Zurich: Piper.). The second edition, containing Rathenow's unchanged text but with only 100 photographs by Hauswald, was published two years later in Dortmund by Harenberg (Die Bibliophilen Taschenbücher, nr. 563.). The work of two young East Germans who existed very much at the edge of the GDR's officially promoted cultural scene, both volumes had been denied publication in the GDR and were confiscated at the Leipzig Book Fair in 1988 and 1989 respectively. It was in 1990, after the demise of the GDR, that the final, completely reworked version of the book was able to appear. It succeeds in evoking a familiar, unglamorous East Berlin which is now rapidly disappearing.

25 **Berlin aus der Luft.** (Berlin from the air.)
Photographs by Günter Schneider, text by Richard Schneider, translated from the German by Ann Robertson. Berlin: Nicolai, 1991. 77p.

An excellent selection of colour photographs offering bird's-eye views of Berlin as it was at the beginning of the 1990s. There is no photograph of what remains of the Berlin Wall, the emphasis being on presenting the city as a single, undivided entity.

26 **Berlin im November.** (Berlin in November.)
Text by Anke Schwartau, Cord Schwartau, Rolf Steinberg, photographs
by Klaus Lehnartz, Dirk Lehnartz, Pressefoto Mrotzkowski, Günter
Peters, Zenit, foreword by Walter Momper. Berlin: Nicolaische
Verlagsbuchhandlung, 1990. 167p.

A collection of black-and-white photographs recording the revolutionary events of
November 1989 in Berlin. The accompanying text is in German, English (translation
by Barbara A. Reeves), and French. Other books of photographs on the same theme,
with German text only, are 9. *November 1989. Der Tag der Deutschen. Eine
Bilddokumentation*, assembled by Bernhard Michalowski, Christine Proske and
Günther Fetzer (Munich: Heyne, 1990. 4th ed. 108p.); 9. *November 1989. Der Tag der
Deutschen* (Hamburg: Carlsen, 1989. 80p.); Klaus Liedtke, ed., *Vier Tage im
November*, with texts by Walter Momper and Helfried Schreiter (Hamburg: Gruner &
Jahr, 1990. 5th ed., 160p.); *Freiheit – schöner Götterfunken. Die glücklichen Tage von
Berlin* (Frankfurt am Main, Germany; Berlin: Ullstein, 1990. 120p.).

27 **Berlin then and now.**
Tony Le Tissier. London: Battle of Britain Prints International
Limited, 1992. 472p. bibliog.

This volume presents a rich variety of black-and-white photographs which tell what is
essentially the story of Berlin in the twentieth-century. Tony Le Tissier, who served in
Berlin as a member of the British Military Government for fourteen years prior to
unification in 1990 and was the British Governor of Spandau prison at the time of
Rudolf Hess' death there in 1987, provides an informative narrative as well as helpful
glosses to the photographs. There is also an exhaustive index by Peter B. Gunn.

Geography

General

28 **Berlin: the spatial structure of a divided city.**
T. H. Elkins, B. Hofmeister.   London, New York: Methuen, 1988.
274p. bibliog.

This scholarly, admirably comprehensive, and well-illustrated study presents a geographer's perspective on a divided Berlin. The book is divided into nine chapters: Berlin as the 'product and victim of history', in Elkins' words; the division of Berlin; the Berlin countryside (including an analysis of the city's water, climate, and vegetation, and of its recreational assets); transport; the city's economy; urban development before 1945; post-war urban development; population; and a concluding chapter on the future. On the basis of his analysis Elkins concludes that, of the two halves of the city, it is East Berlin which probably has the less problematical future. Given his presentation of East Berlin as 'the functioning capital of a state of 16.7 million people, occupying a position of undisputed political, administrative, economic, and cultural leadership' (p. 243) and his more controversial suggestion that West Berlin may be 'no longer an essential component of German life' (p. 251), this was undoubtedly a reasonable enough conclusion in 1988, but it is one which history has since contradicted. Nevertheless, Elkins' findings generally remain as valid today as when they were first written. The book includes numerous photographs, figures, and tables as well as an index.

29 **Berlin (West): eine geographische Strukturanalyse der zwölf westlichen
Bezirke.** (Berlin [West]: a geographer's structural analysis of the twelve
western districts.)
Burkhard Hofmeister. Darmstadt, Germany: Wissenschaftliche
Buchgesellschaft; Gotha, Germany: Haack, 1990. 2nd rev. ed. 322p.
bibliog. (Wissenschaftliche Länderkunden, vol. 8).
The product of impressive scholarship, this volume can be read in conjunction with
that edited by Zimm (q.v.) in order to gain a complete picture for the whole of Berlin.
It is addressed to the specialist geographer.

30 **Berlin und sein Umland: eine geograpische Monographie.** (Berlin and its
environment: a geographical monograph.)
Edited by A. Zimm. Gotha, GDR: VEB Hermann Haack, 1988. 369p.
maps. bibliog.
A geographers' study of Berlin and its environs, this volume concentrates on the
period 1871-1945 as experienced by the whole of Berlin and on the post-1945 period in
East Berlin as the 'capital of the GDR'. Written by geographers from East Berlin's
Humboldt University, this is a book for the specialist. It includes numerous maps,
figures, diagrams, and photographs. After German unification, a revised edition
appeared under the title *Berlin (Ost) und sein Umland* (edited by Alfred Zimm.
Darmstadt, Germany: Wissenschaftliche Buchgesellschaft; Gotha, Germany: Haack,
1990. 3rd rev. ed. 399p. bibliog.).

Districts

31 **Prenzlauer Berg-Tour.** (A tour of Prenzlauer Berg.)
Daniela Dahn. Leipzig, GDR: Mitteldeutscher-Verlag, 1987. 202p.
Published in West Germany as *Kunst und Kohle* (Art and coal.),
Neuwied. FRG: Luchterhand, 1987. 236p. (Sammlung Luchterhand
785).
In what she describes as only the second book ever written on the subject (the first
dating back to 1928), Daniela Dahn explores Prenzlauer Berg, the working-class
district located within a stone's throw of the centre of what used to be East Berlin. At
the heart of her lively narrative is a series of interviews with people of various
backgrounds and ages – among them a representative of the anti-fascist resistance, a
carpenter, a retired cook, a punk, a pensioner who was a neighbour of Käthe Kollwitz,
the director of the abbattoir, a headmistress – whose stories open up before the reader
a rich human perspective on life in the district as it has been lived since the beginning
of the century. Dahn does not shy away from investigating the negative aspects of
Prenzlauer Berg – indeed, one chapter is entitled 'Unpleasant phenomena', while
another sees her as an observer at the trial of the local king of illegal gambling.
Nevertheless, it is disappointing that only half a page of uncritical comment is devoted
to the impact of the Wall on life in the district. Fifty-six black-and-white photographs
are also included. An instructive companion volume is Irene Liebmann's *Berliner
Miesthaus* (Berlin tenement) (Halle, GDR: Mitteldeutscher Verlag, 1982. West
German edition, Frankfurt am Main, FRG: Frankfurter Verlagsanstalt, 1990. 196p.),

9

which contains twenty-nine accounts of visits to the various occupants of one tenement building in a street in Prenzlauer Berg.

32 **Neukölln.**
Felix Escher. Berlin (West): Colloquium, 1988. 105p. bibliog.
(Geschichte der Berliner Verwaltungsbezirke, vol. 3).

To mark the celebration in 1987 of the 750th anniversary of the founding of Berlin, the Historical Commission in Berlin published a series of twelve volumes, each devoted to a different district of West Berlin. Felix Escher's excellent book on Neukölln follows the same pattern as the others, dealing in its first part (p. 9-17) with the present situation in the district and its likely development, and in its second with historical aspects from earliest times through to the post-war period. The other volumes in this useful series are: *Charlottenburg*, by Dieter Schütte (volume 1); *Kreuzberg*, by Heinrich Kaak (volume 2); *Reinickendorf*, by Axel Reibe (volume 4); *Schöneberg*, by Volker Viergutz (volume 5); *Spandau*, by Wolfgang Ribbe (volume 6); *Steglitz*, by Annette Godefroid (volume 7); *Tempelhof*, by Peter Buchholz (volume 8) *Tiergarten*, by Michael S. Cullen (volume 9); *Wedding*, by Klaus Dettmer (volume 10); *Wilmersdorf*, by Hans-Ulrich Kamke and Sigrid Stöckel (volume 11); and *Zehlendorf*, by Jürgen Wetzel (volume 12).

33 **Berlins Straßennamen.** (Berlin's street-names.)
Klaus Katzur. Berlin (West): Haude & Spener, 1987. 236p. bibliog.

This book lists the names of all streets in the twelve districts of West Berlin and adds a brief explanation of the significance of each name. In only a few cases was the author unable to provide such an explanation, either because the local authorities' relevant files were lost or not properly maintained. For a consideration of street-names in eight districts in the eastern part of the city (Pankow, Prenzlauer Berg, Mitte, Friedrichshain, Weißensee, Hohenschönhausen, Lichtenberg, and Hellersdorf), see Günter Nitschke, Ines Rautenberg, Christine Steer, Kurt Wolterstädt, Hermann Zech, foreword by Heinz Knobloch, *Berliner Straßennamen. Ein Nachschlagewerk* (Berlin street names. A reference book.) (Berlin: Christian Links, 1992. 336p.).

34 **Berlin und seine Wappen.** (Berlin and its coats of arms.)
Werner Vogel. Berlin (West); Frankfurt am Main, Germany: Ullstein, 1987. 101p. bibliog.

The coats of arms of Berlin's twenty-three administrative districts are discussed in turn in this illustrated short history.

Maps

35 **Berlin: Bartholomew RV city map.**
Berlin; Gütersloh, Germany; Munich, Stuttgart: Produced for
Bartholomew, a division of HarperCollins Publishers, by RV Reise- und
Verkehrsverlag. [n.d.] Scale 1:27,500.
This is a handy-sized map of unified Berlin. It includes a plan of the underground
railway system and an index of street names.

36 **Berlin, mit Potsdam.** (Berlin, with Potsdam.)
Berlin, Hamburg, The Hague, Paris, London, New York: Falk, 1991.
Scale 1:25,000-1:35,000.
This is a detailed map of Berlin which folds away to pocket size. Includes an index of
street names, additional maps (showing the inner city, outlying areas of Berlin
including parts of the former GDR, and Potsdam), and a list of useful addresses and
telephone numbers. An enlarged version is available for ease of use by those exploring
Berlin by car ('Berlin im Auto'). Falk maps are updated every ten to eighteen months.

37 **Berlin mit Potsdam und Umgebungskarte: Falkplan extra.** (Berlin with
Potsdam: Falkplan extra.)
Hamburg, Berlin; Eindhoven, Netherlands; Antwerp, Netherlands:
Falk, [n.d.] 7th ed. 1:25,000-35,000. (Stadtplan no. 1132).
The reverse side of this handy map includes a map (1:25,000) of eastern Germany from
Prenzlau in the north to Torgau in the south and from Dessau in the west to the Polish
border in the east. There are a further ten smaller maps, including one of Potsdam, as
well as an index of street names.

38 **Großer Stadtplan Berlin.** (Big city plan of Berlin.)
Berlin; Gütersloh, Germany; Munich, Stuttgart: RV Reise- und
Verkehrsverlag, 1990. Scale 1:27,500.
Includes a detailed plan of the centre of West Berlin, a plan of train services in the
city, a list of street names, and details of important addresses. The map is regularly up-
dated.

39 **Berlin und seine Umgebung im Kartenbild nebst Beiträgen zur
Landschafts- und Klimageschichte des Berliner Raumes.** (Maps of Berlin
and its environs, with texts on the history of the landscape and climate of
the Berlin area.)
Edited by Wolfgang Scharfe, contributions by Frank. K. List, Hans-
Joachim Pachur, Wolfgang Scharfe, Paul Schlaak.   Berlin (West):
Colloquium, 1987. 88p. bibliog. (Wissenschaft und Stadt. Publikationen
der Freien Universität Berlin aus Anlaß der 750-Jahre-Feier Berlins,
vol. 2).
This volume, which is the catalogue of an exhibition mounted as part of the
celebrations to mark 750 years of Berlin's history in 1987, demonstrates the

development of Berlin and its environs with the help of maps drawn from the fourteenth to the twentieth centuries.

40   **Die ältesten Stadtpläne Berlins 1652 bis 1757.** (The oldest city maps of Berlin 1652 to 1757.)
        Günther Schulz.   Weinheim, FRG: Acta Humaniora VCH, 1986. 200p. maps. bibliog.

The author's main purpose in this scholarly work is to assemble in as complete a form as possible all the maps of Berlin for the period in question (there are eighty-nine in all) and to date them as precisely as he can. There are excellent illustrations and the maps are indexed.

41   **Planbuch Berlin.** (Street maps of Berlin.)
        Edited by Zitty.   Reinbek, FRG: Rowohlt, 1987. 212p. index.

A series of street maps covering the various parts of Berlin, accompanied by valuable tips for the tourist (sights, restaurants, cinemas, theatres, etc.). Unfortunately, superb eye-sight is necessary in order to be able to read some of the maps!

Geology

42   **Der geologische Aufbau der Gegend von Berlin: zugleich als Erläuterung zur geologischen Karte und Baugrundkarte von Berlin (West) im Maßstab 1:10,000.** (The geological structure of the Berlin area: being also a commentary on the geological map and the foundation soil map of Berlin (West) on the scale 1:10,000.)
        P. Assmann, contributions by O. F. Gandert, G. Siebert, G. Sukopp. Berlin (West): Senator für Bau- und Wohnungswesen, 1957. 142p. bibliog.

This scholarly volume includes the two maps referred to in the title. They are contained in a pocket inside the back cover.

Guide Books

General

43 **Berlin: Berlitz travel guide.**
Text by Jack Altman, photography by Claude Huber.   Lausanne,
Switzerland: Berlitz Guides, 1991/92. 8th ed. 136p. index.

A compact, well-written guide for the tourist who wants to know 'What to see' and
'What to do' in Berlin. It includes a brief introduction to the city, its natives, and their
history, as well as a useful section on eating out (a list of hotels and restaurants is
provided in an appendix). Excellent colour photographs are also included.

44 **Weekend cities: short breaks in 8 popular European cities.**
James Bentley.   London: George Philip, 1988. 224p.

A basic guide to Berlin (p. 64-87) for those with only enough time to sample the city's
most important tourist attractions.

45 **Baedecker's Berlin.**
Marianne Bernhard, Madeleine Cabos, Rainer Eisenschmid, translated
from the German by David Cocking, James Hogarth, Julie Waller,
Crispin Warren.   Basingstoke, England: Automobile Club, 1992. 2nd
ed. 303p.

This superbly produced, informative, and comprehensive guide contains a wealth of
practical tips for the tourist. A pocket inside the back cover contains a useful fold-out
map of Berlin.

46 **American Express pocket guide to Berlin.**
Derek Blyth.   London: Mitchell Beezley, 1992. 144p.

A handy guide which provides the bare essentials on the following topics: Berlin past,
present, and future; basic information; culture, history, and background; planning,

walking, and trips; sights; accommodation; shopping; eating out; nightlife. A section on Potsdam and some German phrases and vocabulary are also provided, as well as an index, a list of street names, and seven maps.

47 **Berlin: Polyglott travel guide.**
Frank Burian, adapted for American readers by Donald Arthur.
Munich: Polyglott, 1990. 64p. index.

Useful short guide with a sensible mixture of general information, practical hints, and commentary on the important sights in Berlin, with a brief note on Potsdam.

48 **Berlin: an English guide to known and unknown treasures.**
Penny Croucher. Berlin (West): Haude & Spener, 1987. 134p.

Based on articles originally written for '*The Berlin Bulletin*' (the newspaper of the British forces stationed in Spandau in north-west Berlin), this highly readable and informative book offers more than a simple rehearsal of the familiar points made in so many guides, instead successfully conveying the stimulating sense of discovery which accompanied the author's own first encounters with Berlin. In exploring the city, the book penetrates well below the surface and therefore retains its value today even though it was written while Berlin was still divided. It is illustrated by numerous black-and-white photographs, but unfortunately there is no map.

49 **Berlin.**
Petra Dubilski. Cologne: DuMont, 1991. 263p. (DuMont Reise-Taschenbücher).

A popular and useful guide for the tourist.

50 **BerlinAtlas für Fahrradfahrer.** (Berlin atlas for cyclists.)
Berlin (West): Fahrradbüro Berlin, 1986. 6th rev. ed. 44p.

A comprehensive guide to the many cycle paths which make Berlin such a friendly city for cyclists. Includes descriptions of nine recommended routes for excursions as well as numerous illustrations.

51 **Berlin.**
Joachim Fait. Munich: Prestel, 1992. 193p. (Prestel Guide).

This pocket-size guide is superbly illustrated and presents its information in a well-structured, easily-digested way which makes the book a pleasure to use.

52 **Berlin.**
Andrew Gumbel. London: Cadogan Books; Chester, Connecticut: Globe Pequot Press, 1991. 260p. bibliog. maps. index. (Cadogan City Guides).

This is a well-written and refreshingly realistic guide, as its opening demonstrates: 'Make no mistake, Berlin is still two cities . . . Berlin is suffering a giant hangover from the Cold War'. It describes nine walks round the city and also includes sections on the sights, food and drink, accommodation, entertainment and night-life, shopping, sports and other activities, travel, history, and a practical A to Z. Finally, there is a note on the German language and a short list of useful words and phrases.

53   **Berlin Brandenburg: ein Architekturführer: an architectural guide.**
Peter Güttler, Joachim Schulz, Ingrid Bartmann-Kompa, Klaus-Dieter
Schulz, Karl Kohlschütter, Arnold Jacoby, translated from the German
by Michael Robinson.   Berlin: Ernst & Sohn, 1990. 357p. bibliog.
This book provides reliable information on and useful insights into the architecture of
Berlin.

54   **Berlin: the rough guide.**
Jack Holland, John Gawthorp.   London: Rough Guides, 1992. 326p.
This no-nonsense guide provides a reliable introduction to the newly united city of
Berlin. Readers looking for colourful photographs, however, would be advised to seek
them elsewhere.

55   **Berlin for young people.**
Edited by Informationszentrum Berlin, translated into English by Mitch
Cohen.   Berlin: Informationszentrum Berlin, 1990. 5th revised and
expanded edition. 160p.
This pocket-sized compendium for the young (and modestly resourced) visitor to
Berlin contains a fund of useful information and maps carefully organised for ease of
reference. Like its attractively produced companion volume *Outlook Berlin* (edited by
Udo Wetzlaugk, translated from the German by Joan Glenn.   Berlin: Infor-
mationszentrum Berlin, 1989. 3rd ed. 96p. Numerous illustrations and photographs,
many in colour), it is available free of charge from the Informationszentrum Berlin, D-
1000 Berlin 12, Hardenbergstraße 20. Also available is a special edition of *Outlook
Berlin* (edited by Uwe Prell, Horst Peter Schaeffer, and Horst Ulrich with the aid of
Ulrike Zieger. [1991?] 39p. maps and tables), which was produced shortly after Berlin,
like the rest of Germany, was unified.

56   **Berlin.**
Thilo Koch.   Munich: Bruckmann, 1991. 152p.
In this colourful volume the excellent photographs of E. Pansegrau are supplemented
by Thilo Koch's lively text, which is presented in both English and German.

57   **Essential Berlin.**
Gabrielle MacPhedran, Adam Hopkins.   Basingstoke, England:
Automobile Association, 1992. 128p.
This is an attractively illustrated, pocket-size guide which gives a lively introduction to
the tourist's Berlin.

58   **Fodor's 92 Berlin.**
Edited by Paula Rackow.   New York: Random House, 1992. 168p.
This is a practical, down-to-earth guide. Its only weakness is that it contains no
photographs.

59 **Berlin and Potsdam.**
Edited by Marion Radkai. London: Robertson McCarta; Munich:
Nelles, 1991. 256p. (Nelles Guides).
This useful guide provides sufficient detail for those who want a succinct introduction
to Berlin but also wish to do more than scratch the surface of the city.

60 **Frommer's budget travel guide: Berlin '92-'93 on $40 a day.**
Beth Reiber. New York, London, Toronto, Sydney, Tokyo,
Singapore: Prentice Hall, 1992. 215p. index. plans. maps. bibliog.
An informative, no-nonsense guide full of practical tips on planning a trip to Berlin,
details of accommodation options, dining possibilities, shopping, sights, walking tours
and excursions, and Berlin at night. Basic phrases and vocabulary in German are also
provided. There are no photographs.

61 **Berlin: two cities under seven flags: a kaleidoscopic A-Z.**
Karin Reinfrank-Clark, Arno Reinfrank. Leamington Spa, England;
New York: Berg, 1987. 254p. index. (Oswald Wolff Books).
This informative but unconvential guide to Berlin and the Berliners is peppered with
lively anecdotes which make it a pleasure to savour, but busy tourists looking for
quick, no-nonsense reference to the basics would be well advised to look elsewhere.
The book is organised alphabetically by topic – from A for 'All Aboard' to Z for
'Zoological Gardens'. Fifty-five illustrations by J. Bettenstaedt are also included.

62 **Berliner Bibliotheken: Erziehungswissenschaften/Pädagogik, Philosophie,
Religion/Theologie.** (Berlin libraries: education/pedagogy, philosophy,
religion/theology.)
Compiled by Heidemarie Schade. Berlin: Colloquium, 1990. 160p.
bibliog.
This is the tenth in a series of volumes prepared by Heidemarie Schade as a guide to
library resources in Berlin (West) for particular subject areas. The previous nine,
which all share the same compiler and publisher, are on *Art and cultural studies* (1981.
101p.); *Social sciences: politics and society* (1981. 88p.); *History* (1982. 113p.);
Language and literature (1983. 116p.); *Law, state and administration* (1985. 127p.);
Economics (1986. 125p.); *Natural sciences* (1987. 138p.); *Engineering sciences and
technology* (1988. 120p.); *Medicine and associated areas* (1989. 131p.). Each volume
includes a list of all the Berlin libraries covering the particular subject area in question
as well as full details of their location, holdings, opening times etc.

63 **Berlin and Potsdam.**
Uwe Seidel, translated into English by Robert van Krieken. Bielefeld,
Germany: Rump, 1992. 312p.
This is a guide which the English-speaking tourist will find useful, although it is a pity
that, with the exception of the attractive cover, it contains only black-and-white
photographs.

64 **Berlin.**
Claire Sharp, photographs by Jean-Claude Mouton. Brentford,
England: Lascelles, 1992. 224p. bibliog.
This is a reliable, up-to-date guide with a wealth of useful information and tips for the
tourist. It is divided into four sections: 'Background', 'Before you go', 'In Berlin', and
'Beyond Berlin'.

65 **Berlin: West-Berlin Ost-Berlin und Potsdam.** (Berlin: West Berlin East
Berlin and Potsdam.)
Michael Stone. Munich, FRG: Prestel, 1989. 200p. index.
maps. (Prestel-Städteführer).
This superbly produced volume contains a veritable mine of information on Berlin's
rich cultural variety. It includes 276 excellent photographs, 150 of them in colour, and
fourteen maps/plans. A plan of the city's railway system can be found on the inside of
the back-cover. Highly recommended.

66 **Berlin.**
Edited by Heinz Vestner. Singapore: Apa Publications, 1989. 339p.
(Insight City Guides).
Compiled by sixteen writers and illustrated with excellent photographs, this guide is
aimed at the casual traveller interested in 'new roadways of discovery off the beaten
track of sightseeing tourism'. There is a good section of practical tips (p. 281-327) and
an index. See also a companion volume by Johanna Behrend entitled *Berlin* (Hong
Kong: Apa Publications, 1992. 129p. Insight Pocket Guides.).

67 **Footloose in Berlin.**
John Walker. Sunderland, England; London: Thomas Reed, 1988.
160p.
A well-written, pocket-size guide which aims to highlight 'the Berlin you might have
missed'. Numerous black-and-white photographs are included.

68 **Berlin city guide.**
Text by John Walker. Glasgow, Scotland: HarperCollins, 1991. 128p.
An inexpensive, pocket-size guide with excellent photographs. It is organized into two
parts, each of which follows an alphabetical sequence of headings. The first deals with
topics such as beaches, churches, excursions, restaurants, shopping, and walks; each
topic is accompanied by its own map for ease of orientation. The second section is an
alphabetical list of information and practical tips.

69 **Berlin zwischen Sekt und Selters.** (Berlin between champagne and soda
water.)
Edited by Axel Wunsch, Stephan Kass, Thomas Schweer. Cadolzburg,
Germany: Ars Vivendi, 1992. 238p.
This volume contains details of 217 bars and cafés in Berlin (forty of them in the
eastern part of the city), ranging from traditional beer-cellars to bistros, jazz cellars,
and hard-rock cafés. It includes the comments of independent inspectors who visited
each establishment incognito.

70 **Berlin: ein Reisebuch in den Alltag.** (Berlin: a traveller's guide to
everyday life.)
Edited by Zitty.   Hamburg, FRG: Rowohlt, 1989. 310p. bibliog.
(Anders Reisen).

Conceived as part of a series entitled *Anders reisen* (roughly: Another way of
travelling), this paperback volume sees itself as an alternative to the more traditionally-
conceived guides to West Berlin. In the main it consists of succinct essays on a variety
of aspects (social, cultural, historical) of West Berlin. Written before the revolution of
1989, the sections on East Berlin are reliable but relatively brief and obviously have in
mind the needs of the tourist intent on a short visit. Apart from its generally lively style
and attractive appearance, the guide's principal distinctive features are the particular
emphasis it gives to 'the scene' (the Berlin of the young, creative, and unconventional)
and the warts-and-all but basically positive approach adopted by the team of
contributors – all of them journalists working for the West Berlin magazine *Zitty*.
There is a useful section of practical tips and addresses, including a plan of the
underground and city train systems (p. 255-306), as well as numerous photographs and
an index. A useful companion volume, which contains detailed maps of the city as well
as essential information in brief for the tourist, is *Anders reisen: Planbuch Berlin*
(Another way of travelling: Street maps of Berlin), edited by Zitty.   Reinbek, FRG:
Rowohlt, 1987.

Seven hundred and fiftieth anniversary

71 **750 years of Berlin: manifesto.**
Ernst Diehl, translated from the German by Intertext Berlin.   Berlin
(East): Panorama DDR, 1985. 77p.

This official manifesto, written by a group of historians headed by Professor Ernst
Diehl, was commissioned by the 'Committee of the German Democratic Republic to
mark the 750th anniversary of Berlin' in 1987.

72 **750 Jahre Berlin: Stadt der Gegenwart: Lese- und Programmbuch zum
Stadtjubiläum.** (750 Years of Berlin: city of the modern age: programme
for the city's anniversary.)
Edited by Ulrich Eckhardt, foreword by Richard von Weizsäcker.
Frankfurt am Main, FRG; Berlin (West): Ullstein, 1986. 352p.

All the events which were officially organized by the Senate of West Berlin to
celebrate Berlin's 750th birthday are published here side by side with sixteen essays by
various authors on the history and importance of Berlin. The volume contains
numerous photographs. See also *750 years Berlin 1987: the programme*, edited by
Harald Jähner and with a foreword by Eberhard Diepgen, (Berlin [West]: Senat, 1987.
348p.).

73   **750 Jahre Berlin: das Buch zum Fest.** (750 years of Berlin: the festival guide.)
Edited by Komitee der Deutschen Demokratischen Republik zum 750-jährigen Bestehen von Berlin.   Berlin (East); Leipzig, GDR: VEB Tourist, 1986. 368p.

This guide covers the impressive programme of cultural events devised by the GDR to celebrate the 750 years of Berlin's history, including a rich succession of concerts, exhibitions, plays, operas, and ballets. Of particular note in the context of East Berlin is the unusually high number of foreign companies and artists invited to take part in the festival.

74   **Topography of terror: Gestapo, SS and Reichssicherheitshauptamt on the 'Prince-Albrecht-Terrain': a documentation.**
Edited by Reinhard Rürup, translated from the German by Werner T. Angress.   Berlin (West): Arenhövel, 1989. 237p. bibliog. index.

The Prince-Albrecht-Terrain, bound by Prinz-Albrecht-Straße (subsequently Niederkirchnerstraße), Wilhelmstraße, and Anhalterstraße and within a stone's throw of Unter den Linden, was the location of the most feared institutions of terror during the Third Reich: the Gestapo, the SS, and the Reich Security Main Office. Heavily damaged by bombing during the Second World War, all the buildings associated with these organizations were flattened in the 1950s and the entire area was then cleared. A lively debate took place in Berlin during the 1980s about the most appropriate way to transform the site into a memorial, but this proved inconclusive and the terrain remains a controversial eyesore to this day. An exhibition planned for the city's 750th anniversary celebrations in 1987 had to be housed in a temporary construction adjacent to the Martin-Gropius-Building. This volume is a record of the material which was assembled for the exhibition and includes 264 black-and-white photographs and eighty-seven translated texts.

Museums

75   **Berlin Museum: Kurzführer: Short guide.**
Dominik Bartmann, Veronika Bendt, (et al.), translated from the German by Shiel Ross.   Berlin (West): Berlin Museum, 1987. 144p.

An excellent short introduction to this museum in Berlin which is devoted to the city's own history. The volume has parallel German and English texts as well as 124 photographs.

76   **The Gemäldegalerie, Berlin: a history of the collection and selected masterworks.**
Compiled by Henning Bock, Rainald Großhans, Jan Kelch, Wilhelm H.
Köhler, Erich Schleier, translated from the German by John Gabriel.
London: Weidenfeld & Nicholson, 1986. 432p. bibliog.

Founded in 1830, the Gemäldegalerie does not boast a large collection of paintings,
but does have an excellent selection of masterpieces which deservedly put it among the
most important galleries in the world. Many of these masterpieces are reproduced in
the present volume, which also contains informative essays by each of the compilers on
various aspects of the collection. In addition, Henning Bock provides a helpful
introduction to the history of the collection (p. 10-35).

77   **The complete catalogue of the Gemäldegalerie, Berlin.**
Compiled by Henning Bock, Rainald Großhans, Jan Kelch, Wilhelm H.
Köhler, Erich Schleier, foreword by Henning Bock, translated from the
German by Ewald Osers.   New York: H. N. Abrams, 1986. 550p.
bibliog.

This catalogue publishes for the first time since the Second World War a complete list
of the holdings of the Gemäldegalerie in Berlin. The inventory is arranged
alphabetically (p. 9-38), but the section of illustrations is arranged by country and
periods (p. 85-550).

78   **Museen in Berlin: ein Führer durch über 80 Museen und Sammlungen.**
(Museums in Berlin: a guide to over 80 museums and collections.)
Forewords by Anke Martiny, Volker Hassemer.   Prestel: Munich,
1989. 2nd rev. ed. 360p.

This handy and attractive guide offers a comprehensive survey of all West Berlin's
major museums and collections (for a relatively short but informative section on
museums in East Berlin, see p. 348-54). It is extremely user-friendly, including details
such as opening times, telephone numbers, and recommended bus and rail
connections. Each entry includes an expert commentary on the museum or collection
in question and includes photographs of some of the most valuable exhibits. A useful
appendix provides full details of selected archives, libraries, cultural institutes,
galleries, dealers in art and antiques, and auction houses. A subject index can be found
on p. 346-7. This volume is highly recommended.

79   **Museum für Verkehr und Technik Berlin: Schätze und Perspektiven: ein
Wegweiser zu den Sammlungen.** (Museum of transport and technology:
treasures and perspectives: a guide to the collections.)
Berlin (West): Nicolai, 1985. 145p. (Berliner Beiträge zur
Technikgeschichte und Industriekultur. Schriftenreihe des Museums für
Verkehr und Technik Berlin, Band 1).

This catalogue of one of Berlin's newest museums (founded in 1983) includes
informative chapters on the Anhalter railway station (of which only a ruin remains
following its destruction in the Second World War – the Museum itself stands on what
was once the station's goods yard); on Berlin's encounter with the motor car (the first
motor-car exhibition in Germany took place in the city in 1897); Berlin's role in the

pioneering of air-travel and in particular the early achievements of Otto Lilienthal in
the 1890s; the growth of Berlin as one of Germany's biggest inland harbours; the
development of public transport in the city; and the birth of Berlin's fire service.

80 **Egyptian Museum Berlin.**
Edited by Heather Dean Wondrausch, foreword and English text by Biri
Fay. Mainz, Germany: Verlag Phillip Zabern, 1990. 4th rev. and
expanded ed. 164p. bibliog.
This scholarly and well-written official guide to the Egyptian Museum contains
excellent colour photographs of about eighty striking exhibits in what is one of the
most distinguished collections in Europe. Some objects were purchased as early as
1698, but the official birth of the Museum was not until 1828 when interest in Egypt
was at its height in Prussia as elsewhere in Europe. The Museum's best known exhibit
is what must probably count as the most famous work of ancient Egyptian art – the
bust of Queen Nefertiti, more than 3,000 years old, a photograph of which adorns the
cover of the guide. Discovered during a famous excavation at Tell el Amarna in 1912,
'Nefertiti' was presented to the Prussian State in 1920 by James Simon, a Berlin
merchant.

The arts

81 **Berlin arts guide.**
Irene Blumenfeld. London: Art Guides Publications, 1986. 147p.
A comprehensive pocket guide to the arts scene in both parts of divided Berlin
covering the visual arts, music, literature (including bookshops and libraries), theatre,
dance, film, and arts festivals. It also includes a section of general information on
Berlin as well as numerous black-and-white photographs.

82 **National Gallery Berlin.**
Matthias Eberle, Lucius Griesebach, Dieter Honisch, Peter Krieger,
Michael Pauseback, Angela Schneider, foreword by Stephan Waetzoldt,
introduction by Dieter Honisch, translated from the German by J. W.
Gabriel. Berlin (West): Druckhaus Tempelhof, 1980. 126p. bibliog.
This standard guide to the National Gallery in Berlin contains six black-and-white and
fifty-three colour plates.

83 **Kunstführer Berlin.** (Art guide to Berlin.)
Birgit Gatermann, Sabine Paqué, translated from the German by Fiona
Short. Berlin: Elefantenpress, 1991. 367p.
This book provides a lively introduction to Berlin's major art galleries and museums
and to the city's plans for future developments in the cultural sphere. An English
summary is included (p. 276-301), as is a section of useful maps (p. 29-49), a list of
addresses, and an index of Berlin artists whose work is exhibited in the city's galleries
and museums.

Special features

84 **Der Reichstag: die Geschichte eines Monumentes.** (The Reichstag: the history of a monument.)
Michael S. Cullen. Berlin (West): Frölich & Kaufmann, 1983. 448p. bibliog.

The main emphasis in this lively history of the Reichstag in Berlin is on its economic and social dimensions, although political, constitutional, architectural and other aspects are by no means ignored. The book includes numerous photographs and illustrations as well as appendices and an index.

85 **Guide book to the Berlin Zoological Garden and its aquarium.**
Edited by Heinz-Georg Klös, translated from the German by Hans Frädrich. Berlin (West): Zoologischer Garten Berlin, 1988. 8th rev. ed. 160p. index.

This attractively produced guide to Berlin's world-famous zoo, illustrated by 147 excellent colour photographs and including a fold-out site-plan, provides an indispensable introduction to the more than 16,000 animals and 1,760 species in the collection. Officially opened on 1st August 1844 as the first zoo in Germany and only the ninth in the world, Berlin Zoo was founded in 1841 when the Prussian King Friedrich Wilhelm IV presented his large pheasantry in the Tiergarten and his collection of animals on the Pfaueninsel (near Potsdam) to the citizens of Berlin. In 1939 Berlin could claim to have the most important zoo in the world, with about 4,000 mammals and birds in some 1,400 species, while the aquarium had 8,300 reptiles, amphibians, fish, and invertebrates in more than 750 species. However, only 91 animals survived the bombing and fighting in Berlin in the last months of the Second World War. After the war the zoo gradually re-established its importance and now attracts almost three million visitors a year.

86 **Das Brandenburger Tor: Brennpunkt deutscher Geschichte./Focus of German history.**
Rainer Laabs, translated from the German by Hild Wollenhaupt. Berlin: Ullstein, 1990. 208p. bibliog.

Laabs provides an interesting introduction to the history of the Brandenburg Gate, arguably the best known symbol of Berlin after the fall of the Wall.

87 **Das Berliner Rathaus.** (Berlin town hall.)
Ralf Melzer. Berlin: Presse- und Informationsamt des Landes Berlin, 1992. 2nd revised and expanded edition. 34p.

From the early 1950s the 'red town hall', as it is popularly known, was home to the city government of East Berlin. On 1 October 1991, however, the Senate of unified Berlin met there for the first time, thus renewing a tradition which goes back to 1869. Melzer's booklet provides an introduction to the building's history and its importance in the political life of the German capital.

88   **Der Kurfürstendamm: Leben and Mythos des Boulevards in 100 Jahren deutscher Geschichte.** (The Kurfürstendamm: life and myth of the boulevard in 100 years of Germany history.)
Karl-Heinz Metzger, Ulrich Dunker.   Berlin (West): Konopka, 1986. 287p. bibliog.

In this well-informed and well-illustrated book the authors set out to provide the first comprehensive history of the Kurfürstendamm, one of the most famous thoroughfares in Berlin and the centre of its western half during the years of the city's post-war division. While taking account of the particular aura which is attached to the Ku'damm (as it is popularly called) today, they go beyond this to show how the street has changed in appearance and function during its history.

89   **Beschreibung der königlichen Residenzstadt Berlin: eine Auswahl.**
(Description of the royal residence Berlin: a selection.)
Friedrich Nicolai, edited by Karlheinz Gerlach.   Berlin (East): Propyläen, 1987. 282p.

Nicolai (1733-1811) was born in Berlin as the son of a prominent publisher and bookseller, in whose footsteps he followed in 1758. He quickly acquired a reputation as a writer of novels, essays, and reviews and as an active participant in the literary and philosophical disputes of the day. The volume offers a representative selection from the book *Beschreibung der königlichen Residenzstädte Berlin und Potsdam, aller daselbst befindlicher Merkwürdigkeiten, und der umliegenden Gegend* (Description of the royal residences Berlin and Potsdam, of all the notable sights to be found there, and of the surrounding area), which Nicolai published in its third revised edition in 1786.

90   **Charlottenburg Palace.**
Edited by Verwaltung der staatlichen Schlösser und Gärten, translated from the German by Henriette Beal.   Hartmann: Berlin, 1989. 8th rev. ed. 109p. bibliog. index.

The official guide to a magnificent palace 'of grandiose baroque character' built at the end of the seventeenth century and named after Sophie Charlotte, the 'philosophical Queen' who, as the second wife of Frederick I, encouraged an intellectual atmosphere at the Berlin court. An informative text is unfortunately marred by some strange English. Thirty-eight black-and-white photographs are also included.

91   **Plötzensee Memorial Berlin.**
Friedrich Zipfel, Eberhard Aleff, Hans Ludwig Schoenthal, Wolfgang Goebel, translated from the German by Margaret Cain.   Berlin (West): Colloquium Verlag, 1989. 22nd amended ed. 31p. bibliog. map.

In 1952 a memorial for the victims of National Socialism was erected in north-west Berlin at the site of Plötzensee Prison (today a juvenile corrective establishment) where some 2,500 people of various nationalities were guillotined or hanged, including eighty-nine of the conspirators involved in the unsuccessful attempt on Hitler's life on 20th July 1944. This short guide includes brief biographies of nineteen representative resistance fighters, numerous photographs and a map.

Flora and Fauna

92 **Naturbuch Berlin.** (Nature book of Berlin.)
Edited by Gruppe Ökologie und Planung. Berlin (West): Nicolai,
1985. 296p.

Addressed to the layman interested in protecting nature, this volume provides a comprehensive guide to the animals and plants found in Berlin. There are 359 illustrations, of which 323 are in colour.

93 **Die Moosflora des Botanischen Gartens Berlin-Dahlem.** (The moss flora of the Botanical Garden in Berlin-Dahlem.)
Mario Menzel. In: *Verhandlungen des Berliner Botanischen Vereins*,
no. 3 (1984), p. 25-62.

A scholarly study of the moss flora in Berlin's celebrated Botanical Garden.

94 **Veränderungen der Moosflora von Berlin (West).** (Changes to the moss flora of Berlin [West].)
Annemarie Schaepe. Berlin (West), Stuttgart: Cramer, 1986. 392p.
bibliog. (Bryophytorum Bibliotheca Bd. 33).

This study aims to meet the need for an up-to-date examination of the moss flora found in West Berlin and thus provide the basis for a comparison with similar studies by earlier scholars. Such a comparison enables appropriate conclusions to be reached on how the moss flora can best be protected in a large city. Given the enviable resources of its Botanical Museum, West Berlin is a suitable place to undertake this kind of study, which the author sees as making a major contribution to the ecology and landscape planning of the city. The volume contains numerous figures and tables, as well as three appendices.

Biographies, Autobiographies, Memoirs and Diaries

95   **An ambassador of peace: pages from the diary of Viscount D'Abernon.**
Viscount D'Abernon, with historical notes by Maurice Alfred
Gerothwohl.   London: Hodder & Stoughton, 1929. 3 vols.

Viscount D'Abernon was British Ambassador to Berlin from 1920 to 1926. The three
volumes of his diary are entitled: 'From Spa (1920) to Rapallo (1922)' (332p.); 'The
years of crisis. June 1922-December 1923' (336p.); 'The years of recovery. January
1924-October 1926' (317p.). The last volume includes personal sketches of Stresemann,
Austen Chamberlain, Carl von Schubert, and Ramsay MacDonald (p. 10-32). As he
relinquished his post, the Ambassador took an optimistic view of developments during
his years in Germany, noting with pleasure that the Franco-German border was, in his
opinion, no longer a subject of heated controversy; '. . . the worst danger-spot in
Europe has been dealt with, and the menace of a new conflagration reduced, if not
exorcised.' (p. 268). His final words, written in October 1926, would ring hollow only a
few years later; 'I have found German statesmen reliable and strong. What higher
praise is there?' (p. 268).

96   **Red Cross and Berlin Embassy 1915-1926: extracts from the diary of
Viscountess D'Abernon.**
Viscountess D'Abernon, with explanatory notes by Patrick Campbell.
London: John Murray, 1946. 152p. map.

The British Ambassador to Germany from 1920 to 1926 was Viscount D'Abernon
(q.v.). These extracts from his wife's diaries deal first with her experiences in France
and Italy as an anaesthetist helping to deal with the wounded of the First World War
(the notes begin in 1916 and not 1915 as suggested by the book's sub-title), and then in
Berlin. She stresses the fact that she has not attempted to tamper with her jottings in
the light of the events of the Second World War. Although she expresses fear that this
might now make her diaries appear 'short-sighted' (p. 141), they do in fact afford some
fascinating insights into Anglo-German diplomatic relations in the 1920s and into the
personalities involved. The book contains an index, a map, photographs, and three
appendices.

97   Hotel Adlon: the life and death of a great hotel.
Hedda Adlon, translated from the German and edited by Norman
Denny.   London: Barrie Books, 1958. 256p.

Situated at Nr. 1 Unter den Linden, in the direct proximity of the Brandenburg Gate,
the Hotel Adlon was founded on 23 October 1907 and survived the heavy bombing of
Berlin in the Second World War as if by a miracle, only to burn to the ground just a
few days after the cessation of hostilities. During its existence it housed leading
statesmen, diplomats, bankers, industrialists, and world-famous celebrities as a matter
of course. Having managed the hotel for many years in partnership with her husband,
Hedda Adlon is able to provide a first-hand, informative, and entertaining memoir
which introduces some of the best-known of these personalities and provides an insight
into an important aspect of Berlin's cultural heritage.

98   **Moses Mendelssohn: a biographical study.**
Alexander Altmann.   London: Routledge & Kegan Paul, 1973. 900p.
bibliog. (The Littman Library of Jewish Civilization).

Altmann's purpose in this scholarly study is to present a detailed picture of
Mendelssohn in strictly biographical terms, observing his life from within the particular
period in which it was set (1726-86) rather than attempting to assess its significance
with the benefit of the historian's hindsight. Described after his death as 'the pride and
ornament' of Berlin, Mendelssohn emerges as a major figure of the Berlin
Enlightenment who was also deeply rooted in Jewish tradition.

99   **Rahel Varnhagen: the life of a Jewess.**
Hannah Arendt, translated from the German by Richard Winston, Clara
Winston.   London: East & West Library, 1957. 222p. bibliog.
(Publications of the Leo Baeck Institute of Jews from Germany).

Largely written before Arendt left Germany in 1933, this excellent study sets out,
according to the author's preface, to narrate 'the story of Rahel's life as she herself
might have told it'. Arendt's aim is to follow as faithfully as possible the course of
Rahel's reflections upon herself rather than to pass judgement on her from some
supposedly higher vantage-point. The volume includes a chronology of Rahel's life
(p. 189-91), a photograph of Wilhelm Hensel's pencil drawing of Rahel as a young girl,
and an appendix with excerpts from Rahel's letters and diaries in the original German
or, occasionally, French.

100   **Days of sorrow and pain: Leo Baeck and the Berlin Jews.**
Leonard Baker.   New York: Macmillan; London: Collier Macmillan,
1978. 396p. bibliog.

Leo Baeck (1873-1956) was a rabbi in Berlin for thirty years and the leader of the
Berlin Jewish community in its encounter with Nazism until 1943, when the Nazis
removed him to Theresienstadt concentration camp. Baker's carefully researched
biography reveals the supreme courage of a distinguished scholar who, first in Berlin
and then in Theresienstadt, refused the opportunity to abandon his flock in order to
save his own life. He became a British citizen in 1950 and died in London on
1 November 1956. The volume includes thirty-two pages of black-and-white
photographs.

101 **Rudolf Virchow: the scientist as citizen.**
Byron A. Boyd.   New York: Garland, 1991. 269p. bibliog.
An informative, critical study of the life and works of the celebrated pathologist who
for many years worked in Berlin's Charité hospital.

102 **My life in politics.**
Willy Brandt, translated from the German by Anthea Bell.   London:
Hamish Hamilton, 1992. 498p.
Willy Brandt was active in Berlin politics from the immediate post-war years; he
became Governing Mayor of the Western half of the city in the autumn of 1957, and
remained in that post until his appointment as Federal German Foreign Minister in the
Grand Coalition government of 1966-69. Originally published in German in 1989 and
here published in abridged form with a new preface by the author, his memoirs make
clear that he regarded himself as 'a politician who learnt his trade in Berlin' (p. 6) and
as someone whose attachment to the city was deep and lasting. Without wishing to
claim too much for his achievements in a long and distinguished career, he nevertheless
takes pride in insisting that he did help to restore the battered image of Berlin in the
post-war years. The book contains a chronology of biographical data (p. 479-82) and
sixteen pages of black-and-white photographs.

103 **German diary.**
Fenner Brockway.   London: Gollancz, 1946. 148p.
This volume is Fenner Brockway's diary of his visit, as a journalist, to the British zone
in Germany for two weeks in April/May 1946, three days of which were spent in
Berlin. The war damage which he finds in central Berlin is, in his view, no worse than
that in central London. He is surprised that the Berliners look better fed and healthier
than the inhabitants of Hamburg but discovers that this is because the food ration in
Berlin, although far below the human-need line, is nevertheless a third higher than in
the British zone. Brockway describes a press conference given by the impressive
Deputy Military Governor, Sir Brian Robertson, as well as meetings with two young
Social Democrat leaders, Franz Neumann and Karl Germer, and with the remarkable
Dr. Wegscheider, head of education in Berlin and Brandenburg before 1933. As a
democratic socialist and an opponent of the totalitarian communism which he accuses
the Soviets of espousing, Brockway reports on the latter's strong-arm methods to try
and push through the fusion of the Communist Party (KPD) and the Social Democratic
Party (SPD) with the aim of ensuring overall communist control. He also expresses his
unease at evidence that young British officers appear to be enjoying an excessively
privileged life, 'a bubbling white froth on the surface of the wretched life which is
Berlin' (p. 70).

104 **Georg Brandes: Berlin als deutsche Reichshauptstadt: Erinnerungen aus
den Jahren 1877-1883.** (Georg Brandes: Berlin as the capital of the
German Reich: memoirs from the years 1877-1883.)
Edited by Erik M. Christensen, Hans-Dietrich Loock, translated from
the Danish by Peter Urban-Halle.   Berlin: Colloquium, 1989. 619p.
bibliog. (Wissenschaft und Stadt. Publikationen der Freien Universität
Berlin aus Anlaß der 750-Jahr-Feier Berlins, vol. 12).
This work by the eminent Danish literary scholar Georg Brandes (1842-1927),
published in Danish in 1885, is here presented in German translation for the first time.

It consists of newspaper reports which were originally written with Scandinavian readers in mind and which convey a richly subjective impression of Berlin during the early Second Empire. The book includes numerous illustrations.

105 **Berlin journal 1989-1990.**
Robert Darnton.   New York: Norton, 1991. 352p.

Robert Darnton is an American Professor of History who happened to spend the academic year 1989-1990 in Berlin and therefore witnessed the turmoil into which that city and Germany as a whole were thrown by the collapse of the GDR and the rest of Eastern Europe. His journalistic account of his experiences takes the form of a series of chronologically ordered, occasionally overlapping essays, some of which originally appeared in abridged form in the journal *The New Republic*. These are supplemented by chapters based on 'chance encounters' in the GDR which are intended to reveal some of the peculiarities of life there. Although somewhat anecdotal in approach, the book is highly readable and does succeed in conveying some of the excitement and uncertainty surrounding Germany's 'peaceful revolution'. Nineteen black-and-white photographs are also included along with an index. For a German version see, *Der letzte Tanz auf der Mauer: Berliner Journal 1989-1990.* (Munich: Hanser, 1991). For another outsider's experiences in Berlin and Germany at the time of the revolution, see the sensitive, diary-like reports of the Dutch writer Cees Nooteboom in his *Berliner Notizen* (translated into German from the Dutch by Rosemarie Still, with photographs by Simone Sassen. Frankfurt am Main: Suhrkamp, 1991. 338p.) Nooteboom was in Berlin from the beginning of 1989 until June 1990 as a guest of the German Academic Exchange Service (DAAD).

106 **Friedrich Schleiermacher: the evolution of a nationalist.**
Jerry F. Dawson.   Austin, Texas; London: University of Texas Press, 1966. 173p. bibliog.

Dawson's study of the famous Berlin theologian Friedrich Ernst Daniel Schleiermacher attempts for the first time to construct the story of the evolution of Schleiermacher's nationalism from his initial attempts to bring about the national awakening of Prussia after its subjugation by Napoleon (1806-11) until his advocacy of a German nationalism (after 1811). Dawson provides a helpful commentary to the nationalist ideas which Schleiermacher expressed in sermons to his congregation in Berlin and to university students, notably those who had volunteered to fight in the war of liberation against Napoleon.

107 **Trail sinister: an autobiography.**
Sefton Delmer.   London: Secker & Warburg, 1961. 423p.

Born in 1904 in Berlin, where his Australian father was first Lecturer in and then Professor of English at the University, Delmer writes interestingly of his childhood there, of his father's internment after the outbreak of war in 1914, and of his appointment in 1928 at the age of twenty-four to head the *Daily Express*'s Berlin bureau where he stayed until 1933 before being moved to Paris. His account, which includes details of meetings with Hitler and Röhm, has all the liveliness and acute observation of the skilful journalist.

108 **Outcast: a Jewish girl in wartime Berlin.**
Inge Deutschkron, translated from the German by Jean Steinberg.
New York: Fromm International Publishing Corporation, 1989. 262p.

These movingly written memoirs describe the experiences of a young Jewish girl in Berlin from the Nazi takeover in 1933 until the end of the Second World War. Now living in Israel, the author reports that her memories of family life, school, friends, and the constant struggle for survival are so powerful that it took her thirty years to be able to put them down on paper. Originally published in German as *Ich trug den gelben Stern* (I wore the yellow star. Cologne: Verlag Wissenschaft und Politik, 1978), the book formed the basis of the play *Ab heute heißt du Sarah: Bilder aus dem Leben einer Berlinerin* (From today your name is Sarah. Scenes from the life of a Berlin woman), written by Volker Ludwig and Detlef Michel. A successful production by Berlin's Grips-Theater in their autumn 1990 season also appeared on German television.

109 **My life.**
Marlene Dietrich, translated from the German by Salvator Attanasio.
London: Weidenfeld & Nicholson, 1989. 243p.; London: Pan Books,
1991. 308p.

Marlene Dietrich was born in Berlin on 29 December 1901 and buried there in 1992 after her death in Paris. She became a star in Hollywood but first rose to fame as Lola-Lola in Josef von Sternberg's classic film *Der blaue Engel* (The blue angel. 1930), one the most brilliant ever produced by UFA at their Berlin studios. In this intelligent and very individual autobiography, Dietrich declares that she had thought the film would be a flop, finding it 'very ordinary and vulgar' (p. 67) – a typically caustic and self-demystifying judgement on her own career. In the most interesting and even moving part of the book she recalls her relatively privileged childhood in Berlin as a particularly happy one despite the death of her father in the closing days of the First World War. She describes with obvious affection her time as a student at the Max Reinhardt Drama School and her experience as a bit-part actress in various Berlin theatres. Her active opposition to Nazism, which earned her the disapproval of so many of her compatriots, she describes as 'the good gut feeling of a Berliner'. The book also contains a chronology of Dietrich's life and an index. After Dietrich's death, one of the earliest and best publications devoted to her was quickly republished: Franz Hessel, *Marlene Dietrich: ein Porträt* (Marlene Dietrich: a portrait. Berlin: Verlag das Arsenal, 1992. 44p.). The most recent biography is by Donald Spoto, *Dietrich* (London, New York, Toronto, Sydney, Auckland: Bantam, 1992. 307p. bibliog.). See too Renate Seydel, *Marlene Dietrich: Chronik eines Lebens in Bildern und Dokumenten* (Marlene Dietrich: chronicle of a life in pictures and documents. Munich: Nymphenburger, 1984. 304p.), which contains 600 photographs illustrating Dietrich's life and background as well as a detailed history of all her roles in film and theatre (p. 299-303). Also worth consulting is *Marlene Dietrich: portraits 1926-1960.* (Introduction by Klaus-Jürgen Sembach, epilogue by Josef von Sternberg, translation of Sembach's foreword by Arthur S. Wensinger and Richard H. Wood. Munich: Schirmer/Mosel; New York: Grove, 1984. 272p. 123 duotone photographs). This contains over a hundred portraits of Dietrich by a series of master photographers, showing how she was both 'an industrial product' (Sembach) but also, thanks to the sheer force of her personality, one of the most enduring.

Biographies, Autobiographies, Memoirs and Diaries

110 **Spandau.**
Jack Fishman. London: Grafton Books, 1989. 532p. bibliog.

Fishman's first book on the seven Nazi leaders – Hess, Funk, Speer, Schirach, Neurath, Doenitz, and Raeder – who were condemned to terms of imprisonment in Spandau at the Nuremberg trials appeared in 1954 under the title *The seven men of Spandau* and became an international bestseller. *Spandau*, an earlier version of which was published in Great Britain in 1986 as *Long knives and short memories* (London: Souvenir. 474p. bibliog.), contains documentary material which, for security reasons, could not be published in the first book. It also makes use of more recently discovered evidence and brings the story to a conclusion with the death of Rudolf Hess in 1987 and the rapid demolition of Spandau gaol in order to prevent it becoming a shrine for Neo-Nazis (a supermarket now stands on the site). Adopting 'fly-on-the-wall' journalistic techniques, the book reports on the day-to-day existence of the prisoners – their gossip, their prison duties, their responsibilities in the prison garden, their preferred reading, problems of health and morale, contacts with their families, their various reactions to the failure of the Third Reich, and so on. It also includes a selection of black-and-white photographs, some of them taken secretly inside the prison and others chosen from the family albums of the seven men. An index is also included.

111 **Souvenirs d'une ambassade à Berlin septembre 1931 – octobre 1938.**
(Memoirs of an embassy in Berlin September 1931 – October 1938.)
André François-Poncet. Paris: Flammarion, 1946. 357p.

As French ambassador to Berlin from 1931 to 1938 François-Poncet is able to offer a fascinating, first-hand account of the Hitler years in Berlin up to the eve of the Second World War.

112 **My four years in Germany.**
James W. Gerard. London, New York, Toronto: Hodder & Stoughton, 1917. 320p.

James Gerard was the Ambassador of the USA in Berlin from 1913 until diplomatic relations were broken off in 1917. His record of these years affords a first-hand view of the war-fever and xenophobia which beset Berlin when the First World War broke out. It also outlines Gerard's persistent attempts to ensure reasonable conditions for prisoners of war in Germany, not least for the civilians held at Ruhleben near Berlin, and to arrange a passage home for American citizens. He deals in some detail with the diplomatic repercussions in Berlin of the sinking of the *Lusitania* in May 1915. Although he has much to say in criticism of the German people and in particular of the German military, he takes a positive view of the Kaiser, finding him 'a most impressive figure' who 'in his black uniform, surrounded by his officers, certainly looked every inch a king' (p. 5). Somewhat surprisingly, Gerard at one point even praises the Kaiser's taste as an architect – not something which is normally held to be one of his strengths. Another to find the Ambassador's approval is the Socialist leader Karl Liebknecht: 'One cannot but admire his courage' (p. 152). Despite all the momentous events he witnessed while in Berlin, the Ambassador admits to finding the city 'rather dull' once its short social season is over. On its inside covers and in a section which follows the main text the volume contains a number of photographs, documents and illustrations. For a critical assessment of Gerard's period as ambassador in Berlin, see Theodore Richard Barthold's dissertation from Temple University, Philadelphia, *Assignment to Berlin: the embassy of James W. Gerard, 1913-1917*, 1981. 445p. bibliog.

113   **Guns and barbed wire: a child survives the holocaust.**
Thomas Geve.   Chicago: Academy Chicago, 1987. 220p.
This is a revised edition of the same author's book *Youth in chains*, which was first
published in 1958. A further edition was published in 1981 (Jerusalem: Rubin Mass.
262p.). The author was born in 1929 on the shores of the Baltic but was living in Berlin
when, as a Jew, he was imprisoned in June 1943. After his liberation in April 1945, he
drew seventy-nine miniature pictures about daily life in Auschwitz, Groß-Rosen, and
Buchenwald, and these were the origins of his book. It tells the harrowing story of
those who, like himself, grew up in concentration camps. The title of the book is taken
from a line in 'The song of the peat-bog soldiers' the full text of which is included, in
the author's English translation, in an appendix (p. 216).

114   **Passages from Berlin: recollections of former students and staff of the
Goldschmidt Schule.**
Edited by Steve J. Heims.   White Plains, New York: M. Phiebig,
[1987?]. 213p.
This volume contains a collection of essays, autobiographical stories, and reminiscences of people who were pupils or members of staff at a German-Jewish school in
the Grunewald area of Berlin between 1935 and 1939 and had been forced to emigrate
by the rabid anti-semitism prevalent in Germany at that time.

115   **. . .ich soll dich grüßen von Berlin. 1922-1932: Berliner Erinnerungen
ganz und gar unpolitisch.** (. . .Berlin sends its greetings. 1922-1932:
entirely unpolitical memoirs.)
Fred Hildenbrandt, edited post mortem by two friends.   Munich:
Ehrenwirth, 1966. 266p.
Fred Hildenbrandt was editor of the features section *(Feuilleton)* of the *Berliner
Tageblatt*, one of Berlin's leading newspapers, between 1922 and 1932. In his memoirs
he tells of his encounters with some of the most important people he met during what
he calls Berlin's great years, including his editor-in-chief Theodor Wolff, the theatre-
critic Alfred Kerr, the actresses Henny Porten, Marlene Dietrich, Lilian Harvey,
Carola Neher, and Greta Garbo, the dancers Mary Wigman, Gret Palucca, Josephine
Baker, Isadora Duncan, and Valeska Gert, and the actors Heinrich George and Hans
Albers. The volume adopts a lively, anecdotal approach which makes for easy reading.

116   **Gropius: an illustrated biography of the creator of the Bauhaus.**
Reginald Isaacs.   Boston, Massachusetts; Toronto, London: Little,
Brown & Company, 1991. 344p. bibliog.
First published in a two-volume German edition in 1983-84 (Berlin[West]: Gebr.
Mann), this book is the first biography of Gropius to have appeared in English. Berlin-
born Gropius is noted in particular as the founder of the Bauhaus. His involvement
with the Bauhaus in its various phases is fully explored, chapter five being devoted to
the years in Berlin (1928-34) which followed his resignation from his position as
director. The volume includes a detailed chronology of Gropius' life (p. 330-2) as well
as a wealth of photographs.

Biographies, Autobiographies, Memoirs and Diaries

117 **George Grosz: art and politics in the Weimar republic.**
Beth Irwin Lewis. Madison, Wisconsin; London: University of
Wisconsin Press, 1971. 328p. bibliog.

Born in Berlin in 1893, the artist Grosz spent most of his adult life in the city before
emigrating to the United States eighteen days before Hitler became chancellor in 1933.
This book skilfully tells the story of Grosz's controversial career in Berlin while
admitting that – because of Grosz's own reticence in the early years, the destruction of
his private records in Berlin, and his subsequent tendency to falsify the record of his
time in Germany – any reconstruction must remain fragmentary. A useful account of
Grosz's development as a man and as an artist can be found in Hans Hess' liberally
illustrated study *George Grosz* (New Haven, Connecticut; London: Yale University
Press, 1985. 2nd ed. 272p. bibliog.). This contains a biographical table and a list of
Grosz's exhibitions from 1920 to 1974. Also worth consulting are M. Kay Flavell,
George Grosz: a biography (New Haven, Connecticut; London: Yale University Press,
1988. 352p. bibliog.); Martin Kane, *Weimar Germany and the limits of political art: a
study of the work of George Grosz and Ernst Toller,* (Beverley, North Humberside:
Hutton, 1987. 226p. bibliog.); and Serge Sabarsky, *George Grosz: the Berlin years*
(New York: Rizzoli, 1985. 253p. bibliog.). The latter includes a contribution by
Grosz's widow, Marty Grosz. Grosz's fascinating autobiography, in which he admits
that there is much that he has deliberately chosen not to tell, appeared under the title
The autobiography of George Grosz: a small yes and a big no (Translated by Arnold J.
Pomerans. London, New York: Allison & Busby, 1982. 246p.). The same volume was
also published as *A small yes and a big no: the autobiography of George Grosz*
(Feltham, England: Zenith, 1983. 246p.).

118 **Heimweh nach dem Kurfürstendamm: aus Berlins glanzvollsten Tagen
und Nächten.** (Homesick for the Kurfürstendamm: from Berlin's most
glittering days and nights.)
PEM (=Paul Erich Marcus). Berlin (West): Blanvalet, 1952. 236p.

The author had to leave Berlin in 1933 when Hitler came to power, and the beginning
of the book finds him returning for the first time in 1948. This gives him the
opportunity to recall, in a series of anecdotes, many of the people who played a central
role in Berlin's colourful cultural life in the years before the Nazi takeover. Erich
Carow, Alfred Kerr, Erik Charell, Fritz Kortner, Egon Erwin Kisch, Billy Wilder, and
Carola Neher are just some of the major figures who feature in PEM's lively, if not
always entirely reliable recollections. Another equally rich source of information on
leading personalities in the Berlin of the 1920s is Max Krell, *Das alles gab es einmal*
(There was a time) (Frankfurt am Main, Germany: Scheffler, 1961. 362p.).

119 **Slow fire: Jewish notes from Berlin.**
Susan Neiman. New York: Schocken, 1992. 307p.

Susan Neiman, an American Professor of Philosophy and a Jewess, lived in West
Berlin from 1982 to 1988. Her book is a very personal, diary-like account of her
experiences in the city.

120 **Walter Benjamin.**
Julian Roberts. London; Basingstoke, England: Macmillan, 1982.
250p. bibliog.
Benjamin was born in Berlin on 15 July 1892 as the son of well-to-do Jewish parents.
Although he was a prolific writer, he published very little during his lifetime, and it is
only since the 1950s that he has been recognised as a major philosopher. Roberts
provides a general critical account and an authoritative interpretation of his work.

121 **Mies van der Rohe: a critical biography.**
Franz Schulze. Chicago: University of Chicago Press, 1985. 227p.
bibliog.
This recent biography of Mies van der Rohe, an architect who has left his indelible
mark on the face of contemporary Berlin, is both readable and informative. Also
recommended are Philip C. Johnson, *Mies van der Rohe* (London: Secker & Warburg,
1978. bibliog.), originally published in 1947 on the occasion of an exhibition of Mies
van der Rohe's work at the Museum of Modern Art, and Werner Blaser, *Mies van der
Rohe. The art of structure* (Translated by D. Q. Stephenson. London: Thames &
Hudson, 1965. 227p.).

122 **Ernst Reuter: ein Zivilist im kalten Krieg.** (Ernst Reuter: a civilian in
the Cold War.)
Hannes Schwenger. Munich, Zurich: Piper, 1987. 107p. bibliog.
(Serie Piper Porträt).
Schwenger's book provides a useful short introduction to the life of Ernst Reuter
(1889-1954), who became West Berlin's mayor during the air blockade of 1948-49 and
remained a determined fighter for the people of the divided city until his early death.
A fuller treatment can be found in Willy Brandt and Richard Löwenthal's *Ernst
Reuter: ein Leben für die Freiheit: eine politische Biographie* (Ernst Reuter: a life for
freedom: a political biography) (Munich, 1957). See also Klaus Harpprecht, ed., *Ernst
Reuter: ein Leben für die Freiheit: eine Biographie in Bildern und Dokumenten* (Ernst
Reuter: a life for freedom: a biography in pictures and documents) (Munich, 1957).

123 **Last train from Berlin.**
Howard K. Smith. New York: Knopf, 1942. 359p.; London: Cresset
Press, 1942. 266p.
After a period at Oxford as a Rhodes scholar, the American journalist and broadcaster
Howard K. Smith was a correspondent in Berlin from January 1940 until December
1941, for United Press (UP) and then as a radio correspondent for the Columbia
Broadcasting System (CBS). Describing himself as the last American to get out of
Germany while still a free man (Germany declared war on the United States just after
he had left for Switzerland), Smith devotes the bulk of his book to providing a personal
record of the changes which took place in Berlin and Germany in the second half of
1941 after the outbreak of hostilities between the Soviet Union and Hitler's forces.
This is a lively, journalistic account, which is enriched by Smith's perceptive
observation of the impact of war on the Berliners.

124 **The papers of General Lucius D. Clay: Germany 1945-49.**
Edited by Jean Edward Smith. Bloomington, Indiana; London:
Indiana University Press, 1974. 2 vols. bibliog.

This collection of General Clay's papers, which amounts to 746 items, includes the editor's brief but helpful annotations as well as a detailed index. Clay was the administrator of US occupied Germany from 1945-49 and author of *Decision in Germany* (q.v.).

125 **Karl Friedrich Schinkel: a universal man.**
Edited by Michael Snodin, translated from the German by Patricia
Crampton, Anthony Vivis, Eileen Martin. New Haven, Connecticut;
London: Yale University Press in association with The Victoria and
Albert Museum, 1991. 219p. bibliog.

Karl Friedrich Schinkel (1781-1841) was the architect responsible for many of Berlin's finest, neo-classical buildings. These include the Neue Wache (New Guardhouse, 1814-15), the Schauspielhaus (Theatre, 1818-21, here described as 'the first architecturally significant theatre building to be built in Germany' [p.20]), and the Altes Museum (1823-30). Schinkel was also a brilliant designer as well as an accomplished painter. This handsomely illustrated volume includes a detailed catalogue of the 160 items, most of them on loan from Berlin museums, which were shown in a comprehensive exhibition of Schinkel's work held at London's Victoria and Albert Museum from 31 July to 27 October 1991 (p. 88-207). This was the first Schinkel exhibition ever to take place in the English-speaking world. The seven essays which accompany the catalogue justify the sub-title of the volume by pointing up the full range of Schinkel's genius; 'Karl Friedrich Schinkel: a universal man' (Peter Betthausen); 'Schinkel the artist' (Helmut Börsch-Supan); 'Schinkel's buildings and plans for Berlin' (Gottfried Riemann); 'Schinkel and Durand: the case of the Altes Museum' (Martin Goalen); 'Royal residences on the Havel' (Hans-Joachim Giersberg); 'Schinkel's architectural theory' (Alex Potts); 'Art and industry' (Angelika Wesenberg). A further section of the book contains twenty-four splendid old photographs of Schinkel's major buildings, a number of which have tragically been destroyed (p. 64-87). There is also a detailed chronology of Schinkel's life (p. 208-213).

126 **Inside the Third Reich: memoirs.**
Albert Speer, translated from the German by Richard Winston, Clara
Winston, introduction by Eugene Davidson. London: Weidenfeld &
Nicolson, 1970. 596p. bibliog.

Following his condemnation as a war criminal at the Nuremberg Trials Albert Speer was imprisoned in Spandau jail in the north-west of Berlin until October 1966. During this time he produced more than 2000 pages of memoirs which he subsequently reworked with the aid of documents preserved in the Federal Archives in Koblenz. These are of interest not least for the insight they afford into what Hitler regarded as the greatest assignment he could give to Speer as his favourite architect – an appointment as Inspector General of Buildings for the Renovation of the Capital, responsible for turning Berlin into a capital which would surpass even Paris and Vienna. Speer was charged *inter alia* with the construction by 1950 of a new avenue three miles long and 130 yards wide, an arch of triumph 400 feet high, and 'a huge meeting hall, a domed structure into which St. Peter's Cathedral in Rome would have fitted several times over' (p. 74) and in which there would be standing room for a hundred and fifty thousand people. Fortunately, nothing came of the megalomaniac

Biographies, Autobiographies, Memoirs and Diaries

schemes apart from the planting of tens of thousands of deciduous trees: 'Of the whole vast project for the reshaping of Berlin, these deciduous trees are all that have remained' (p. 78). The volume includes an index as well as numerous photographs of models and sketches prepared by Hitler and Speer in pursuing their project. See also Albert Speer, *Spandau. The secret diaries* (translated from the German by Richard and Clara Winston. London: Collins, 1976. xii and 465p. bibliog. index); M. Schmidt, *Albert Speer. The end of a myth* (London: Harrap, 1984, 276p.) and Leon Krier, *Albert Speer. Architecture 1932-1942* (Brussels: AAM Editions, 1985).

127 Judgement in Berlin.
Herbert J. Stern. New York: Universe Books, 1984. 384p. bibliog.

On 30 August 1978 an East German waiter, Detlef Tiede, hijacked a Polish aeroplane on a flight from Warsaw to East Berlin's Schoenefeld airport, forcing it to land at Tempelhof airport in the United States sector of West Berlin. As a result, Tiede, his accomplice Ingrid Ruske, her daughter Sabine, and eight other passengers on the flight were able to begin a new life in the West. However, the Hague and Tokyo conventions of 1978 required that those who committed piracy in the air should be prosecuted or extradited. For the first time since its establishment on paper in 1955 the United States Court for Berlin had to be called into session and a United States judge for Berlin appointed. This was Herbert J. Stern, and his book is a detailed account, told in the third person and frequently quoting verbatim from the minutes of the court proceedings, of all the circumstances surrounding this most remarkable escape story and the legal and moral complexities to which it gave rise.

128 Wilhelm von Humboldt: a biography.
Paul R. Sweet. Columbus, Ohio: State University Press, 1978. 2 vols. Volume 1, 1767-1808; Volume 2, 1808-35; bibliog.

Described by Lord Acton as 'the most central figure in Germany' in his time, Wilhelm von Humboldt (1767-1835) was an outstanding statesman, man of letters and scholar. He is today best known as the founder of the university in Berlin which bears the Humboldt name and as a major influence on the development of humanistic education in Germany in the nineteenth century. Sweet's impressively comprehensive and balanced study is the authoritative, standard biography in English.

129 Hess: a tale of two murders.
Hugh Thomas. London, Sydney, Auckland, Toronto: Hodder & Stoughton, 1988. 2nd rev. ed. 223p. bibliog.

In 1947 Rudolf Hess, Adolf Hitler's Deputy, was imprisoned in Spandau jail with six other prominent Nazis, including Albert Speer and Baldur von Schirach (q.v.). When the latter were released in 1966, Hess remained the solitary prisoner in Spandau until his death in 1987. Hugh Thomas, a British surgeon who had some responsibility for Rudolf Hess in 1972-73, became convinced that prisoner 7 was not Hess at all but an impostor 'thrust upon, or infiltrated by, the British in 1941' (p. 11). He arrived at this view when he discovered no scar wounds on the prisoner's body, whereas Rudolf Hess had been seriously wounded in the chest in the First World War. He concludes that the real Hess was murdered under mysterious circumstances and replaced by the impostor who arrived by plane in Scotland on an unlikely peace mission in May 1941 and was immediately arrested. The book was originally published in 1979 under the title *The murder of Rudolf Hess*. The change of title is explained by Thomas' assertion that the impostor did not commit suicide on 17th August 1987, as the official version would have it, but that he too was murdered. In seeking to cover this up the British government became guilty of 'one of the most disgraceful crimes in history' (p. 195). In his book *My father Rudolf Hess* (translated from the German by Frederick and Christine Crowley. London: W. H. Allen, 1986, 414p.), on the other hand, Hess' son Wolf Rüdiger clearly believes that prisoner 7 *was* his father, that he was a martyr and 'an innocent person' (p. 338), that his imprisonment was an 'atrocity' and 'one of the most malicious judicial murders of all time' (p. 12), and that the allies, having spurned the offer of peace which Hess carried with him to Scotland, probably used his incarceration as a means 'to conceal the fact that at the very least they were accessories to the continuation of the war, a war which did not reach its full measure of horror until after 1941' (p. 11).

130   **The Goebbels diaries: the last days.**
      Edited, introduced and annotated by Hugh Trevor-Roper, translated
      from the German by Richard Barry.   London: Secker & Warburg,
      1978. 368p. bibliog.

Goebbels became Nazi Gauleiter of Berlin in 1926 at the age of twenty-eight and was elected a Berlin deputy in the Reichstag two years later. In his introduction to this edition of the diaries which Goebbels kept between February and April 1945, Hugh Trevor-Roper quotes Hitler as saying of his Gauleiter's achievement in the capital: 'When he started, he found nothing particularly efficient as a political organisation to help him; nevertheless, in the literal sense of the word, he captured Berlin.' (p. xix). As John Keegan has pointed out in what may be regarded as a companion volume (see *The Goebbels Diaries 1939-41.* Translated and edited by Fred Taylor, foreword by John Keegan. London: Hamish Hamilton, 1982. 490p. index) the diaries might be called *Inside Hitler's capital* (by analogy with Albert Speer's *Inside the Third Reich*, [q.v.]), since this was the centre from which Goebbels wielded his influence for almost twenty years. For a revealing biography, see Roger Manvell and Heinrich Fraenckel, *Dr. Goebbels. His life and death* (London, Melbourne, Toronto: Heinemann, 1960. 329p. bibliog.). The volume has an index, numerous photographs, and appendices listing the chief events in Goebbels' life and showing a plan of the Führerbunker in Berlin.

131   **Berlin under the new empire: its institutions, inhabitants, industry,**
      monuments, museums, social life, manners, and amusements.
      Henry Vizetelly.   London: Tinsley Brothers, 1879. Reprinted New
      York: Greenwood Press, 1968. 2 vols.

Vizetelly describes his book as the result of several prolonged visits to Berlin, the first in 1872. His aim is to provide an accurate picture of what he calls 'a city out of the regular highway of continental travel' which is bound to increase in importance: 'Of the great Germanic body, Berlin is today at once the head and the heart, for in all that relates to the new Empire, it is Berlin that thinks, conceives, frames, organizes and commands'. Vizetelly is an observant, well-informed, entertaining and seemingly indefatigable narrator. He can also be perspicacious, as when passing judgement on Bismarck's attempts to stamp out socialism: 'Outwardly Socialism has been pretty well cleansed from the body politic of the German Empire, but in reality it has only been driven deeper into the system, and we all know the ultimate result of this mode of treatment'. Both volumes have an appendix which brings some of the preceding material up to date. They are illustrated by more than 400 engravings from designs by German artists, including one of Bismarck in his study. This work is highly recommended.

132   **Zoo Station: adventures in East and West Berlin.**
      Ian Walker.   London: Martin, Secker & Warburg, 1987. 329p.;
      London: Sphere Books, 1988. 329p. (Abacus).
A reporter for *The Observer*, Walker spent the mid-1980s (1984-87) in Berlin before
moving to Nicaragua. His account of that period is highly personal in nature,
combining the honesty of a private diary with the journalist's wish to make sense for
others of the experiences which Berlin offers.

133   **The shrinking circle: memories of Nazi Berlin, 1933-1939.**
      Marion Freyer Wolff.   New York: UAHC Press, 1989. 133p. bibliog.
The author was born in Berlin in 1925, the second daughter of the Jewish owner of a
small factory which manufactured buttons and buckles. Her book describes her
personal experiences as a child in Nazi Berlin from 1933 until her emigration to the
United States in 1939.

134   **When time ran out: coming of age in the Third Reich.**
      Frederic Zeller.   Sag Harbour, New York: Permanent Press, 1989.
      205p.
This volume contains the author's memoirs of his childhood in Berlin during the Hitler
era. It covers the period until his emigration to Holland and ends on the eve of his
departure for England.

History

General and miscellaneous

135 **Bistum Berlin: Kirche zwischen Elbe und Oder mit tausendjähriger Vorgeschichte.** (Diocese of Berlin: church between the Elbe and the Oder with a thousand-year pre-history.)
Hubert Bengsch. Berlin (West): Stapp, 1985. 215p. bibliog.

The history of the Catholic Church in Berlin, particularly since the founding of the present diocese in 1930, forms the focus of this book. It was originally written for publication in the GDR and appears here in a licenced edition. Its author is the brother of Cardinal Bengsch, who was Bishop of Berlin for eighteen years from 1961 and advised on the writing of the book up until his death in 1979.

136 **Berlin: eine Stadt wie keine andere.** (Berlin: a city like no other.)
Bernt Engelmann. Munich: Bertelsmann, 1986. 320p. bibliog.

This is a very personal, journalistic account of Berlin's history by one of her own sons. What makes the city like no other, in Engelmann's eyes, is its youth, vitality, and lack of respect for rank and authority. These are hardly deep insights, but their assertion perhaps helps to explain why Engelmann's text remains fresh and lively where it is not always profound or original. Thirty illustrations accompany the text.

137 **Wanderings through Berlin by the Spree and Havel.**
Theodor Fontane, edited by Wolfgang Boehler, translated from the German by Robin Crompton. Heidelberg, FRG: Edition Europäische Kulturstätten, 1968. 40p. bibliog. index.

Contains a short selection from Fontane's writings in which he describes Berlin and its immediate environs as they were in the 1860s and 1870s. Sensitively translated, the book also includes black-and-white photographs of appropriate nineteenth-century paintings and engravings.

138 **Die Chronik Berlins.** (Berlin chronicle.)
     Edited by Bodo Harenberg. Dortmund, Germany: Chronik Verlag,
     1991. 2nd rev. ed. 640p. bibliog. maps.
Produced originally in 1986 to mark Berlin's 750th anniversary, this enormous volume
covers Berlin's history from the beginnings to the present day. It includes contributions
by Heinrich Albertz, Helmut Börsch-Supan, Michael Erbe, Alfred Kerndl, Joachim
Nawrocki, Hans J. Reichhardt, Wolf Jobst Siedler, Peter Steinbach, Werner Vogel,
and Sybille Wirsing. It also contains over 1500 photographs, mostly in colour, as well
as maps and tables.

139 **Berlin 1848: das Erinnerungswerk des Generalleutnants Karl Ludwig
     von Prittwitz und andere Quellen zur Berliner Märzrevolution und zur
     Geschichte Preußens um die Mitte des 19. Jahrhunderts.** (Berlin 1848:
     the memoir of Lieutenant General Karl Ludwig von Prittwitz and other
     sources on the March revolution in Berlin and on the history of Prussia
     in the middle of the nineteenth century.)
     Edited and with an introduction by Gerd Heinrich. Berlin (West),
     New York: de Gruyter, 1985. 518p. bibliog. (Veröffentlichungen der
     Historischen Kommission zu Berlin, vol. 60; Source Books, vol. 7).
Prittwitz was in command of government troops in Berlin during the 1848 revolution
against King Frederick William. His record of the events in which he was a major
participant is published here in its entirety for the first time. Heinrich's learned
introduction outlines with exemplary clarity the political factors which prevented
earlier publication and provides a historical framework within which the importance of
Prittwitz's record can be assessed. The volume includes a map (contained in a pocket
inside the back cover) showing the revolutionary situation in Berlin on 18 and 19
March 1848.

140 **Berlin: Königsresidenz Reichshauptstadt Neubeginn.** (Berlin: royal
     residence, capital of the Reich, new beginning.)
     Martin Hürlimann. Zurich; Freiburg im Breisgau, Germany: Atlantis,
     1981. 328p.
A highly readable history of Berlin for the general reader, illustrated with 341 fine
photographs. An index and chronological table are also included.

141 **Der Wandervogel: es begann in Steglitz.** (The Wandervogel youth
     movement: it began in Steglitz.)
     Edited by Gerhard Ille, Günter Köhler. Berlin (West): Stapp, 1987.
     304p. bibliog.
This collection of essays by a total of nine contributors deals with the Wandervogel
youth movement from its origins in 1895 until its demise with Hitler's coming to power
in 1933. The volume concentrates on the factors which might explain why the
movement developed when it did and why it originated in Steglitz, a district of Berlin.
Particular attention is paid to the leaders of the movement, to the social origins of its
earliest members, and to the role played by girls. There are also informative chapters
on the songs and music inspired by the movement, and on the impact of the First

World War and the rise of fascism. The volume includes a fine selection of photographs and illustrations.

142 **Berliner Wassertürme.** (Berlin water towers.)
Stefan Karner, Peter J. Wichniarz.   Berlin (West): Ernst & Sohn,
1987. 72p. bibliog.

Water towers, many of them built in the nineteenth century and resembling in appearance the towers of medieval castles, are a characteristic feature of Berlin's cityscape. This volume provides an excellent introduction to the history of the water towers and the problems which industrial archaeologists face in ensuring their preservation. It also contains thirty-eight photographs, eight of them in colour.

143 **Berlin: the eagle and the bear.**
John Mander.   London: Barrie & Rockliff, 1959. 193p.

In this consideration of Berlin's past from the time of the Great Elector's accession in 1640, Mander finds much to admire in the city's history, although this does not prevent him from introducing his subject as 'almost certainly the ugliest capital city in Europe' (p. 1). He admits that his narrative reflects his own prejudices, 'too much literature, too little economics'. Nevertheless, this is a well-written account which can be read with profit even today. The eagle of the title was the symbol of Prussia, and the bear is the symbol of Berlin.

144 **Berlin in Geschichte und Gegenwart: Jahrbuch des Landesarchivs
Berlin. 1990.** (Berlin in history and in the present: yearbook of the
Land archives of Berlin. 1990.)
Edited by Hans J. Reichhardt.   Berlin: Siedler, 1990. 672p. bibliog.

This volume forms part of an annual series which has appeared since 1982. It contains scholarly essays on specific aspects of Berlin's history, as well as an assessment of Berlin theatre and critical reviews of Berlin's cultural life as a whole in 1989.

145 **Berlin 1675-1945, the rise and fall of a metropolis: a panoramic view.**
Alexander Reissner.   London: Oswald Wolff, 1984. 175p.

This is a lively history of Berlin for the non-specialist reader. It covers the period from the defeat of the Swedish army by the Great Elector in 1675 until the end of the Second World War, and reaches beyond the standard political history by including interesting sections on subjects such as early department stores in Berlin, the house of Aschinger, and the Hotel Adlon. In addition to an index the volume also contains a chronological table and thirty-two photographs.

146 **Kleine Berlin-Geschichte.** (Short history of Berlin.)
Wolfgang Ribbe, Jürgen Schmädeke.   Berlin: (West): Landeszentrale
für politische Bildungsarbeit, 1988. 270p. bibliog.

Written to coincide with the 750th anniversary of Berlin in 1987, this volume aims to provide the general reader with an up-to-date, comprehensive study of Berlin's history. The text is a model of clarity and is accompanied by a wealth of well-chosen illustrations, including colour photographs, maps, and tables. A fuller account can be found in Ribbe's two-volume *Geschichte Berlins* (History of Berlin) (Munich: Beck, 1987. bibliog.) For an East German view of Berlin's history, written for the general reader and enlivened with numerous illustrations, see Hans Prang and Horst Günter Kleinschmidt, *Mit Berlin auf du und du. Erlesenes und Erlauschtes aus 750 Jahren Berliner Leben* (On familiar terms with Berlin. 750 years of Berlin life) (Leipzig, GDR: Brockhaus, 1980. 192p. bibliog.). In this volume, East Berlin is celebrated as the capital city of the GDR, and West Berlin is notable by its absence from the text.

147   **Berlin: the dispossessed city.**
      Michael Simmons.   London: Hamish Hamilton, 1988. 263p. bibliog.
Although Berlin's history is normally taken to date back at least 750 years, this lively account by a well-known British journalist begins in 1871, the point at which the previously provincial city became an imperial capital almost overnight. The fact that it did so on the basis of victory in war is seen by Simmons as a principal reason underlying the calamities and traumas to come. He is clearly fascinated by Berlin's colourful history but does not make exaggerated claims for the city, saying that, for all its bustle and conviviality, it is essentially a prosaic city which lacks the special quality of excitement which gives others their greatness. His description of Berlin as dispossessed is a reference to its division after 1961. This state of dispossession had been unexpectedly overcome within two years of the book's publication, so Simmons' book may be regarded as the last full-length history of Berlin to have been written in English against the background of the Wall. By contrast, the later, German edition, which appeared under the title *Deutschland und Berlin. Geschichte einer Hauptstadt 1871-1990* (translated from the English by Meinhard Büning. Berlin: Argon, 1990. 330p.), was able to take the fall of the Wall into account.

From the earliest times to 1918

148   **Exerzierfeld der Moderne: Industriekultur in Berlin im 19.**
      Jahrhundert. (Practice ground of modernism: industrial culture in
      Berlin in the nineteenth century.)
      Edited by Jochen Boberg, Tilman Fichter, Eckart Gillen.   Munich:
      Beck, 1984. 403p. bibliog.
This is the first of two volumes devoted to the development of Berlin's industrial culture during the past two centuries (the second, with the same editors and publishers, appeared in 1986 under the title *Die Metropole: industriekultur in Berlin im 20. Jahrhundert* [The metropolis – Industrial culture in Berlin in the twentieth century.]: 403p. bibliog. 335 illustrations, of which nineteen are in colour). The first volume, which has 495 illustrations of which fourteen are in colour, traces the city's growth from almost rural modesty into what the editors, citing Mark Twain, term a 'European Chicago'. The second moves from the ambitious dynamism of the late Wilhelminian era to the tragedy of post-war division. History has certainly vindicated the editors' view, however, that Berlin has the potential to become a major city again, even if, 'for the time being, the city is still living off and with its myths' (p. 9).

41

149 **Colonialism, neocolonialism, and the anti-imperialist struggle in Africa: Marxist studies on the Berlin Conference 1884-85.**
Edited by Thea Buttner, Hans Ulrich Walter. Berlin (East): Akademie Verlag, 1984. vi, 114p. bibliog. (Asia, Africa, Latin America. Special Issue: 13).
Although Berlin cannot look back on a long tradition of staging international conferences (unlike London, Vienna and Paris), the so-called Congo Congress of 1884-85 – along with the Berlin Conference of 1878, the conference of the four superpowers in 1954, and the 1991 meeting of Foreign Ministers as part of the Conference on Security and Cooperation in Europe – certainly belongs in this category. This volume presents the GDR's Marxist view of the conference's significance.

150 **The Berlin West African conference 1884-1885.**
Sybil Eyre Crowe.   Westport, Connecticut: Negro Universities Press, 1970. 249p. bibliog.
Originally published in 1942 by Longman, Green & Company of New York, this scholarly study concentrates not on the importance of the Berlin West Africa conference as a landmark in international law (which the author believes has been much exaggerated) but on its political and diplomatic significance. Crowe argues that the conference must be seen as 'at once the epitome of, and the index to the outcome of' the Anglo-German colonial quarrel of 1884-85 and its corollary, the Franco-German entente of the same year (p. 6). In addition to an excellent index, the volume contains three maps.

151 **Berlin und sein Umland: zur Genese der Berliner Stadtlandschaft bis zum Beginn des 20. Jahrhunderts.** (Berlin and its surroundings: on the genesis of Berlin's urban landscape up to the beginning of the twentieth century.)
Felix Escher.   Berlin (West): Colloquium, 1985. bibliog. (Einzelveröffentlichungen der Historischen Kommission zu Berlin, Bd. 47. Publikationen der Sektion für die Geschichte Berlins, Bd. 1).
A detailed, scholarly investigation of the process by which Berlin developed as an urban landscape between the middle ages and the 1920s. It is well illustrated and indexed.

152 **Lost Berlin.**
Susanne Everett.   London, New York, Sydney, Toronto: Hamlyn, 1979. 208p. maps. index. (A Bison Book).
An attractively-produced book which looks back at the Berlin of Bismarck, the Weimar Republic, and the Third Reich. Many of the book's numerous photographs are from the Federal German Archives in Coblenz.

153 **Bismarck, Europe, and Africa: the Berlin Africa conference 1884-1885 and the onset of partition.**
Edited by Stig Förster, Wolfgang J. Mommsen, Ronald Robinson.
Oxford, New York, Toronto: Oxford University Press, 1988. 569p.
bibliog.
This volume assembles thirty scholarly essays, all originally delivered as papers at an international conference held in Berlin-Tegel in 1985 to mark the Africa conference's centenary. It reflects the great divergence of views among historians about the importance of the Berlin Africa conference and goes some way towards correcting the relative neglect which the conference has suffered among historians.

154 **Berliner Leben 1900-1914: eine historische Reportage aus Erinnerungen und Berichten.** (Berlin life 1900-1914: a historical reportage from memoirs and reports.)
Edited by Dieter Glatzer, Ruth Glatzer. Berlin (West): Verlag das Europäische Buch, 1986. 2 vols. bibliog.
The editors present a selection from the writings of contemporaries which documents the political, social, economic and cultural aspects of Berlin's development in the first years of the twentieth century up to the outbreak of the First World War. The book was first published by Rütten & Loening in East Berlin in 1986. It gives special stress to the exploitation of the working classes which, the editors argue, was a major feature of the era. The volume also contains numerous photographs.

155 **Jewish high society in old regime Berlin.**
Deborah Hertz. New Haven, Connecticut; London: Yale University Press, 1988. xiv and 299p. ill. bibliog.
This scholarly volume is an assiduously researched, eminently readable social history of Berlin's salons between 1780 and 1806. This period is known as the Rahel Era after Rahel Varnhagen, one of the Jewish women whose salons promoted Jewish social emancipation and also helped break down the traditional barriers between noble and commoner in Germany. The civilizing influence of the salons was brought to an abrupt end in 1806 by Napoleon's conquest of Prussia. Seeking to answer the question 'Who came to the Berlin salons, and why?', Hertz constructs a collective biography of 417 female and male intellectuals in Berlin, of whom 100 (a third of them women) attended at least one salon during the Rahel Era: 'The point of the book is to show how the social origins, occupations, friendships, love affairs, and intellectual work of the hundred guests propelled them and did not the other 317 intellectuals into salons' (p. 20). What Hertz finds particularly fascinating about the salons is 'that they provided a public cultural stage for Jewish women at a time when Jewish men had not yet achieved their characteristically high level of participation in German intellectual life' (p. 148). Her findings confirm Ingeborg Drewitz's view (in her book *Berliner Salons: Gesellschaft und Literatur zwischen Aufklärung und Industriezeitalter*, Berlin, 1965) that the salons were the first major milestone in the emancipation of German women. An illuminating biography of the salonière who gave the period its name is Hannah Arendt's *Rahel Varnhagen. The Life of a Jewess* (q.v.).

156   **A history of Prussia.**
H. W. Koch.   London, New York: Longman, 1978. 326p. bibliog.
Berlin was the capital of Prussia before it became the capital of a newly unified
Germany in 1871. In this comprehensive, balanced history of the Prussian state (which,
in his view, effectively came to an end in 1871), H. W. Koch provides a scholarly
account of the historical context within which Berlin's rise to prominence as a major
political centre in Europe took place.

157   **Imperial Berlin.**
Gerhard Masur.   New York: Basic Books, 1970. 353p. bibliog.;
London: Routledge & Kegan Paul, 1971. 353p. bibliog.; New York:
Dorset Press, 1989. 353p. bibliog. maps.
A native of Berlin, Gerhard Masur was forced into American exile by the rise of the
Nazis. When he returned in the mid-1960s, he discovered that 'what is now called
Berlin bears no resemblance to the old imperial city' and in fact reminded him much
more of Chicago or Iowa City (p. 3). He therefore terms his beautifully written book a
study in archaeology which aims to bring to life the vanished world of 1871-1918. At its
heart is an analysis of the process by which the parochial residential and garrison town
of the nineteenth century became, after the unification of Germany under Bismarck,
one of the great urban centres of the West. The volume also includes twelve pages of
photographs. In his lively book *Berlin: Schicksal einer Weltstadt* (Berlin: fate of a
metropolis) (Munich, Berlin [West]: Biederstein, 1958), the journalist Walter Kiaulehn
sets out like Masur to evoke a vanished past which he nevertheless regards as 'eternal
and indestructible'. He concentrates on the period 1871-1933 and produces what he
calls 'a beautiful carousel of Berlin life'. In addition to numerous black-and-white
photographs, the book includes an appendix containing four town plans from the
thirteenth to the nineteenth centuries.

158   **The Congress of Berlin and after: a diplomatic history of the Near
Eastern settlement 1878-1880.**
W. N. Medlicott.   London: Frank Cass, 1963. 2nd ed. 442p. bibliog.
Originally published in 1938 (London: Methuen), Medlicott's excellent study argues
that the Congress of Berlin (1878), presided over by Bismarck, succeeded in producing
a paper settlement of the troublesome Near Eastern question but that the crisis in fact
continued for a further three years until the signature of the Three Emperors' Alliance
Treaty in June 1881. The book is based mainly on diplomatic correspondence in
Austrian and British foreign office archives, in the Russian embassy in London, and in
private collections.

159   **Ernst Dronke: Berlin.**
Edited, and with a foreword by Rainer Nitsche.   Darmstadt, FRG;
Neuwied, FRG: Luchterhand, 1974. 429p.
This only slightly abbreviated reprint of a volume originally published in 1846
(Frankfurt am Main: Literarische Anstalt J. Rütten) contains Ernst Dronke's critique
of the 'despotism' of money and the egoism of the rich in Berlin society. An ally of
Marx and Engels and an early champion of communist ideas, Dronke saw the only
means of overcoming socio-economic injustice in promoting the political enlightenment
of the people. He discerned in the weavers' uprising in Silesia and the strikes of 1844
first signs of popular resistance to social and political oppression. His book is therefore

described by Nitsche as socialist reportage on the development of early capitalism in Germany as seen in the historically new phenomenon of a large and expanding city, Berlin. Unsurprisingly, the book was at once banned in Prussia (it was nevertheless available elsewhere in Germany) and Dronke was persecuted by the Prussian police. Arrrested, he was held in custody for four months before being condemned to two years' imprisonment, but he was able to flee to Brussels after rather more than a year. In 1852 he went into permanent exile in London, eventually dying in Liverpool in 1891.

160 **Frederick the Great.**
Alan Palmer, introduction by Elizabeth Longford.   London: Weidenfeld & Nicolson, 1974. 231p. bibliog. (Great Lives).

A balanced, comprehensive assessment of 'Old Fritz', the legendary eighteenth-century ruler who turned Berlin into the capital of a major European power able to claim at least an equal voice with the archaic Habsburg empire in the affairs of the continent. A classic and highly readable study (first published in 1947) remains G. P. Gooch, *Frederick the Great. The ruler, the writer, the man* (Hamden, Connecticut: Archon Books, 1962. bibliog. index). Gooch presents Frederick as 'a unique and many-sided personality, at once fascinating and repulsive' who 'by almost superhuman efforts hoisted Prussia into the rank of the Great Powers and unwittingly paved the way for a united Germany under the aegis of Berlin'. Gerhard Ritter's *Frederick the Great. A historical profile* (translated, with an introduction by Peter Paret. Berkeley, California; Los Angeles: University of California Press, 1970. 207p. index), which is based on lectures he delivered at the University of Freiburg in 1933 and 1934, sees Frederick above all as exemplifying the rational, prudent use of state power, an intepretation which implicitly cautioned against the dangerous emotionalism of modern totalitarianism as personified in Germany's new leader, Adolf Hitler. For a recent view of Frederick's life as a soldier, see Patrick Duffy, *Frederick the Great. A military life* (London, Melbourne; Henley, England: Routledge & Kegan Paul, 1985. bibliog. index). For a comprehensive history of the Prussian state, see H. W. Koch, *A history of Prussia* (London, New York: Longman, 1978. 326p. bibliog.) (q.v.).

161 **The German revolution of 1918: a study of German socialism in war and revolt.**
A. J. Ryder.   Cambridge, England: Cambridge University Press, 1967. 304p. bibliog.

An authoritative account of a half-completed revolution which Ryder likens to the 1848 revolution in France: 'Berlin's Spartacus Week was the analogue of the June Days in Paris, and Noske the counterpart of Cavaignac.' (p. 1). Ryder argues that the fundamental reason for the revolution's failure was the split among the three main Socialist groups. The volume includes numerous photographs and an index.

162 **Berlin und Frankreich 1685-1871.** (Berlin and France 1685-1871.)
Pierre-Paul Sagave.   Berlin (West): Haude & Spener, 1980. 281p. bibliog.

Sagave investigates the powerful influence which France exercised for a hundred years on the cultural life of Berlin, beginning with the impact of the 6000 Huguenot refugees who were welcomed in Prussia following the Revocation of the Edict of Nantes (1685). He draws attention to the fact that all the heirs to the Prussian throne from the end of the seventeenth century to the beginning of the nineteenth were tutored by Huguenots. This period of French influence reached its peak under Frederick the Great. After

Frederick's death in 1786 and particularly after the French Revolution of 1789, Berlin's view of France become more critical and was characterized by a spirit of rivalry which culminated in the Franco-Prussian War (here reflected mainly through the war correspondence of Theodor Fontane). Sagave's account stops at the point at which the old admiration for things French turned to hatred, a state of affairs which largely persisted until after the Second World War. The book contains numerous photographs and also a chronological table (p. 277-81).

163 **Gold and iron: Bismarck, Bleichröder, and the building of the German empire.**
Fritz Stern. New York: Alfred Knopf; London: George Allen & Unwin, 1977. 620p. bibliog; Harmondsworth: Penguin, 1987. 620p. bibliog. (A Peregrine Book).

As Fritz Stern notes in his introduction to this impressive work of scholarship, over 7,000 works have appeared about Bismarck but this is the first study of Gerson Bleichröder, the Jewish banker who was born in Berlin in modest circumstances in 1822, rose to a position of enormous wealth and influence, and become the first Prussian Jew to be ennobled without converting to Christianity. With the help of thousands of hitherto unused letters and documents, Stern demonstrates for the first time the importance of Bleichröder's role as the chancellor's banker and as his frequent confidant for over thirty years. In his dealings with Bleichröder Bismarck is revealed as a man who in both the public and the private sphere fully understood the significance of money and who recognised even in his celebrated and much studied diplomacy the value of economic weapons as instruments of policy. The statesman and the banker are seen by Stern as the representative men of the age in which Berlin and Germany rose to unprecedented eminence. The link between Bleichröder's Berlin bank, with its headquarters in Behrenstraße, and the Bismarck family continued until the 1930s. It was closed by the Nazis in 1938 as part of the process of Aryanization, but a new bank bearing the name Arnhold and S. Bleichröder was later established first in London and then in New York. The volume contains numerous photographs and an excellent index.

164 **The culture of science in Frederick the Great's Berlin.**
Mary Terrall. *History of Science*, vol. 28, part 4 (1990), p. 333-64.

Taking the Berlin Academy of Sciences as a particularly important setting in which certain features of Enlightenment culture were played out, Mary Terrall examines the Academy's role within the Prussian state as it was built up by Frederick the Great. For Frederick, the Academy was both 'a fitting accoutrement of enlightened monarchy' (p. 336) and an important strategic resource in his efforts to strengthen the state. Terrall pays special attention to the work of Pierre-Louis Maurois de Maupertuis, the Frenchman who was designated as the Academy's 'perpetual president' in 1776 and who put into place an academic ideology which exactly reflected the hierarchical structures characteristic of Frederick's thinking. The article discusses Maupertuis' efforts to establish the Academy as a congenial home for the study of metaphysics in general and of a metaphysically grounded 'least action mechanics' in particular, the latter being compared and contrasted with the reductive mechanics favoured by d'Alembert and the Paris Academy.

The Weimar Republic (1918-33)

165   **Culture and society in the Weimar Republic.**
Edited by Keith Bullivant.   Manchester, England: Manchester
University Press, 1977. 205p. bibliog.

Of particular interest among the eleven essays contained in this volume are Herbert
Scherer's 'The individual and the collective in Döblin's *Berlin Alexanderplatz*' (p. 56-
70), Hugh Ridley's 'Tretjakov in Berlin' (p. 150-65), and Ronald Taylor's 'Opera in
Berlin in the 1920s: *Wozzeck* and *The Threepenny Opera*' (p. 183-89).

166   **How to be happy in Berlin.**
John Chancellor.   London: Arrowsmith, 1929. 204p.

Chancellor's guide-book presents Weimar Berlin as an attractive place for an English
tourist to find himself: 'In six months in Berlin my impression of the Germans is they
are a kindly, sentimental people, who seem to have a marked liking, admiration and
respect for the English' (p. 10). He admonishes English patriots to forget the war and
let bygones be bygones. Apart from anything else (he adds), to do otherwise is to risk
damaging trade. Despite his determined optimism, Chancellor has to admit that Berlin
is not a beautiful city, but it does have a youthful and high-spirited atmosphere which
distinguishes it from London and Paris. The reader looks here in vain for any sense of
the political tensions and social problems which were to lead to the downfall of the
Weimar Republic only a few years later. The volume includes a fold-out street-map of
Berlin (affixed to the inside of the back cover), an introduction to basic words and
expressions in German, and information on shops, restaurants etc.

167   **Bertolt Brecht's Berlin: a scrapbook of the twenties.**
Wolf von Eckardt, Sander L. Gilman.   London: Abelard, 1976. xix
and 170p. bibliog.

First published in 1975 in Garden City, New York by Anchor Doubleday, this
excellent volume succeeds in evoking the atmosphere of Berlin between the World
Wars by combining a lively, well-researched text with a judicious selection of almost
300 photographs, many of them previously unpublished. There are informative and
carefully illustrated chapters, for example, on intellectual life in its various aspects, on
architecture, on sports and on the seedier side of Berlin's moral condition. However,
the title is somewhat misleading (Brecht is only one of a number of major figures
whose life in Berlin is explored), and the chapter on 'Youth' deals with the importance
of various youth movements (Wandervogel, Arbeiterjugend, Freischar, Hitlerjugend)
in Germany in general rather than specifically in Berlin.

168   **Before the deluge: a portrait of Berlin in the 1920's.**
Otto Friedrich.   New York: Harper & Row, 1972. 418p. bibliog.

This is an impressively wide-ranging, well-informed, and lively history of Berlin during
the Weimar Republic. It contains twenty-four pages of photographs and illustrations.
Other editions have been published by Michael Joseph (London, 1974) and by Fromm
(New York, 1986).

169 **Weimar culture: the outsider as insider.**
Peter Gay. Harmondsworth, England: Penguin, 1974. 222p. bibliog.
In Gay's brilliant study of the complex flowering of Weimar culture (1918-33) Berlin emerges as the inescapable centre (p. 7) and as a magnet attracting leading figures from other parts of Germany: 'The old Berlin had been impressive, the new Berlin was irresistible (. . .) Berlin was the place for the ambitious, the energetic, the talented' (p. 134-5). The book also includes twelve pages of black-and-white photographs and was reprinted in 1981 by Greenwood Press, London (205p. bibliog.).

170 **1930: das steinerne Berlin: Geschichte der größten Mietskasernenstadt der Welt.** (1930. Berlin, city of stone: history of the biggest rent-barracks city in the world.)
Werner Hegemann, foreword by Walter Benjamin. Brunswick, FRG; Wiesbaden, FRG: Vieweg, 1988. 4th ed. 344p. (Bauwelt Fundamente 3).
This edition of Hegemann's classic study is, apart from a few minor excisions and the addition of Benjamin's short essay as a foreword, identical to the original edition of 1930. Hegemann recognizes contemporary Berlin's achievements as a wealth-creating centre, pointing out that it has only 7 per cent of the population of Germany but provides 16 per cent of all income tax, 25 per cent of corporation tax, 13 per cent of value-added tax, and so on. However, he condemns Berlin's poor quality of housing, insisting that not a Prussian minister, as hitherto, but a representative of local government in Berlin should be given responsibility for this area. He points to the example of London as worthy of imitation. His book closes with the hope that Berlin will turn its attention to meeting at least the most urgent needs in housing.

171 **The Weimar chronicle: prelude to Hitler.**
Alex de Jonge. New York, London: Paddington Press, 1978. 256p. bibliog.
In seeking to evoke the spirit of Weimar Germany, de Jonge chooses the approach not of an analytical historian but of a chronicler who brings together 'an assembly of voices: extracts from diaries, newspaper reports, eyewitness accounts, memoirs and reminiscences which have been largely allowed to speak for themselves' (p. 6). The volume contains numerous photographs and a chronology of events between 1918 and 1933.

172 **Berlin in der Weimarer Republik.** (Berlin in the Weimar Republic.)
Annemarie Lange. Berlin (East): Dietz, 1987. 1,134p. bibliog.
Taken together with Lange's previous books on Berlin's recent past – *Das Wilhelminische Berlin* (Wilhelminian Berlin) (Berlin [East]: Dietz, 1967) and *Berlin zur Zeit Bebels und Bismarcks* (Berlin at the time of Bebel and Bismarck) (Berlin [East]: Dietz, 1972) – this immense volume presents a history of the city over the last hundred years from a pronounced Marxist-Leninist point of view. Numerous illustrations are also included.

173 **Weimar: a cultural history.**
Walter Laqueur. New York: G. P. Putnam's Sons, 1976. 308p.
bibliog. (Capricorn Books).

Although this well-written introductory survey of what the author in his introduction
calls 'for better or worse, the first truly modern culture' is deliberately not 'limited to
those who frequented certain cafés within a stone's throw of the *Gedächtniskirche* in
Berlin', it does include perceptive analysis of the cultural scene in Berlin. In particular,
a chapter entitled *'Berlin s'amuse'* offers a persuasive overview of popular culture in
the city at a time when Berlin was the entertainment capital of Europe.

174 **The Berlin police force in the Weimar Republic.**
Hsi-Huey Liang. Berkeley, California: University of California Press,
1970. 252p. bibliog.

Liang's main aim is to analyse the part played by Berlin's police force in the failure of
Weimar democracy. This is enriched by thirty-two interviews which he conducted in
the autumn of 1962 with former police officials, details of whom are included in an
appendix. The study, which includes maps and illustrations, also appeared (with some
revisions) in German as *Die Berliner Polizei in der Weimarer Republik* (Translated by
Brigitte Behn, Wolfgang Behn. Berlin [West]; de Gruyter, 1977. 232p. bibliog.)
(Veröffentlichungen der Historischen Kommission zu Berlin, vol. 47).

175 **Beating the fascists? The German communists and political violence
1929-33.**
Eve Rosenhaft. Cambridge, England; London, New York; New
Rochelle, New York; Melbourne, Australia; Sydney: Cambridge
University Press, 1983. 273p. bibliog.

The author's purpose is to investigate why, towards the end of the Weimar Republic,
Communists in German cities were involved in often brutal warfare with their
opponents, particularly the National Socialists. Her case-studies concentrate on events
in Berlin. Three chapters (p. 111-66) deal in detail with a particularly violent episode
there in 1931 when taverns frequented by Nazi stormtroopers were the focus of attack;
with the experience and culture of violence among Berlin's working-class; and with the
possible socio-economic determinants of violence as exemplified in the biographies of
some Berlin street-fighters.

The Third Reich and the Second World War (1933-45)

176 **The official report of the XIth Olympiad Berlin.**
Edited by Harold M. Abrahams. London: British Olympic
Association [1937]. 254p.

The official report of the British Olympic Association, which includes numerous black-
and-white photographs, contains all the essential details of the various sporting
competitions held at the 1936 Olympic games in Berlin. It mentions with particular

warmth the hospitality of the games' German hosts and the award to several British athletes of 'the order of the "*Olympia-Ehrenzeichen*", the first decoration to be created in Germany since the [Weimar] Republic' (p. 33). Nevertheless, a clear indication is given of the political tensions surrounding the games, as when the report notes with diplomatic restraint: 'It was a little unfortunate that no uniformity of saluting was agreed upon by the International Olympic Committee. The French team giving the Olympic salute, so similar to the Nazi form of salutation, received a tumultuous reception. The British contingent with their "eyes-right" met with almost complete silence' (p. 35).

177   **Das Tagebuch der Hertha Nathorff: Berlin-New York: Aufzeichnungen 1933-1945.** (The diary of Hertha Nathorff: Berlin-New York: notes 1933-1945.)
Edited and introduced by Wolfgang Benz.   Munich, FRG: Oldenbourg, 1987. 212p. bibliog. (Schriftenreihe der Vierteljahreshefte für Zeitgeschichte, vol. 54).

Hertha Nathorff, a niece of Albert Einstein and of the Hollywood film producer Carl Laemmle, was a doctor with the Red Cross in Berlin before she emigrated first to England (in 1939) and then to the United States (in 1940). A large part of her original diaries for 1933-1939 was lost en route to the USA and therefore had to be reconstructed from notes and from memory. Nevertheless, this work remains a remarkable record of the experiences of a Berlin Jewess during the Third Reich.

178   **We survived: fourteen histories of the hidden and hunted of Nazi Germany.**
Eric H. Boehm.   Santa Barbara, California; Denver, Colorado; Oxford: ABC-Clio, 1985. 321p.

The majority of the fourteen moving stories of resistance to Nazism which this book tells concern people - famous and ordinary, Jews and gentiles, men and women – who lived through the war in Berlin. They came to Eric Boehm's attention immediately after the war when he was working for the US Military Government in Berlin and got to know over fifty persons who had struggled to survive while standing up to Nazism wherever they dared. The book was first published in 1949 by Yale University Press and then again by Clio Press in 1966. This reprint edition includes a new epilogue by Eric Boehm, an index, and two maps.

179   **Bombers over Berlin: the RAF offensive November 1943-March 1944.**
Alan W. Cooper.   Wellingborough, England: Patrick Stephens, 1989. 2nd ed. 319p. bibliog.

A full account of the RAF's assault on Berlin as the Second World War entered its final stages. In Cooper's view, Bomber Command's controversial sorties made a major contribution to costing Germany the war, pinning down many men, guns, and fighters otherwise certain to have been used at the Russian front and, later, in Normandy: 'These men, guns, and aircraft could have made a vital difference and changed the course of history' (p. 217). They also brought production of war materials in the capital to a virtual standstill. Originally published in 1985 (London: Kimber), the volume contains an index, numerous illustrations, and a section of appendices.

180　**Hitler's games: the 1936 Olympics.**
　　Duff Hart Davis.　London: Century, 1986. 256p. bibliog.
This is a sound account of the Olympic games which took place in Berlin in 1936 and which Hitler hoped would reflect glory on Germany and the Nazi movement. His calculation was thwarted, however, by the success of the outstanding black American athlete, Jesse Owens. This book is also published by Coronet (Sevenoaks, England. 1988. 287p. bibliog.). For a thoughtful and at times provocative account see Richard D. Mandell, *The Nazi Olympics* (New York: Macmillan, 1971. 316p. bibliog.; London: Souvenir Press, 1972. 316p. bibliog.; Urbana, Illinois: University of Illinois Press, 1987. 316p. bibliog.). Also recommended is Judith Homes, *Olympiad 1936. Blaze of glory for Hitler's Reich* (New York: Ballantine Books, 1971. 160p. bibliog.). For an analysis of Leni Riefenstahl's film of the games, see Cooper C. Graham, *Leni Riefenstahl and Olympia* (Metuchen, New Jersey; London: Scarecrow Press, 1986. 323p. bibliog. [Filmmakers, 13]).

181　**Berlin calling: American broadcasters in service to the Third Reich.**
　　John Carver Edwards.　New York; Westport, Connecticut; London:
　　Praeger, 1991. 239p. bibliog.
Edwards' study presents profiles of eight Americans who served Germany's Second World War propaganda effort on Radio Berlin: Jane Anderson (alias the Georgia Peach); Max Otto Koischwitz (alias Mr. O. K.); Robert H. Best (alias Mr. Guess Who); Douglas Chandler (alias Paul Revere); Donald Day; Frederick Wilhelm Kaltenbach; Constance Drexel; and Edward Leopold Delaney. For a discussion of the activities of Lord Haw-Haw, the British 'radio traitor' who became similarly infamous for his broadcasts for Nazi Berlin, see J. A. Cole's *Lord Haw-Haw and William Joyce: the full story* (New York: Farrar, Straus & Giroux, 1964).

182　**The road to Berlin.**
　　John Erickson.　London: Weidenfeld & Nicolson, 1983. 877p. bibliog.
This is the second volume in Erickson's monumental study, *Stalin's war with Germany*, the first volume being *The road to Stalingrad* (London: Weidenfeld & Nicolson, 1975. Reprinted 1977. 594p. bibliog.). It presents a detailed analysis of the Soviet Union's struggle with Hitler's forces from the end of the Stalingrad campaign to the battle for Berlin. Erickson bases his work on his reading of what he terms 'a mighty mountain of material' (p. 789), much of it found in Soviet sources otherwise inaccessible to or largely ignored by Western scholars.

183　**Target Berlin: mission 250: 6 March 1944.**
　　Jeffrey Ethell, Alfred Price.　London, New York, Sydney: Jane's,
　　1981. 212p. bibliog.
On 6 March 1944 the US 8th Air Force mounted its first full-scale daylight assault on Berlin. Sixty-nine bombers and eleven escorting fighters were lost in the course of the day's fighting – more than on any other day in the 8th Air Force's history. This book tells the story of what happened as seen through the eyes of over 160 Americans and Germans who participated in this battle.

184 **Berlin underground 1938-1945.**
Ruth Andreas Friedrich, translated from the German by Barrows
Mussey, with an introductory note by Joel Sayre.   New York: Henry
Holt, 1947. 312p.

During the period of Nazi rule in Germany Ruth Andreas Friedrich was a member of a
small but courageous resistance group centred in the Steglitz district of Berlin. Known
by the code-name *Onkel Emil* (Uncle Emil), it had about two dozen members. It co-
operated with a small communist group without itself having a clear political profile
beyond its anti-Nazism. The author's foreword begins with the ringing declaration
'This book does not pretend to be a work of art; it is simply the truth'. In essence, that truth
is that some Germans – the author talks about thousands upon thousands – found their
consciences would not let them go into exile during the Nazi period. They chose to stay in
order to try and ensure that 'at least not all the intended outrages might be carried out' and
that in this way something be done to rescue the reputation of Germany. Also published in
1948 in London by Latimer House under the title *Berlin underground 1939* [sic]-*1945*.
254p., the book has been translated into French (1966), Dutch (1966), Hebrew (1967)
and Hungarian (1975). The English translation was republished in New York in 1989 by
Paragon House and numerous editions have appeared in Germany, both East and West
the success of which encouraged Suhrkamp to publish the author's diaries of the
immediate post-war years, *Schauplatz Berlin. Tagebuchaufzeichnungen 1945 bis 1948*
(The scene is Berlin. Diaries 1945-1948. Afterword by Jörg Drews. Frankfurt am Main
FRG: Suhrkamp, 1985. 2nd ed. 286p.). An American edition was published under the
title *Battleground Berlin: diaries 1945-1948* (translated by Anna Boerresen, afterword by
Jörg Drews. New York: Paragon House, 1990. 261p.). In Drews' view, these diaries
document Berlin and Germany's moral and political failure to make a new start after the
war. For a fascinating account of life in Germany and particularly Berlin from 1932 until
1945, see Christabel Bielenberg's perceptive memoir *The past is myself* (London: Corgi.
1992. 287p.). Originally published in 1968 (London: Chatto & Windus), it reveals the
author's close association with resistance circles and deals with her husband's arrest after
the failed attempt on Hitler's life on 20th July 1944 as well as with her own interrogation by
the Gestapo. The book was the basis of the memorable television serial *Christabel*, which
was written for the BBC by Dennis Potter.

185 **Strafjustiz in rechtloser Zeit: mein Ringen um Menschenleben in Berlin
1943-45.** (Criminal justice in lawless times: my struggle for human lives
in Berlin 1943-45.)
Hans von Godin.   Berlin: Berlin Verlag Arno Spitz, 1990. 205p.

This book chronicles the efforts of a distinguished lawyer, Hans von Godin, to save
human lives in Berlin during the last years of the Second World War – not least that of
his own father, a prominent lawyer himself.

186 **Das erwachende Berlin.** (Berlin awakens.)
Joseph Goebbels.   Munich: Eher, 1934. 184p.

This book, which is dedicated to Horst Wessels, consists of a foreword by Goebbels
and a selection of photographs showing the National Socialist view of Berlin and its
recent history. Goebbels depicts Berlin as a quick-thinking, ruthless city in which only
the tough and independent-minded can survive. He claims that it has been won back
from the Marxists and the Jews by men willing to lay down their lives in what had
seemed to many to be a pointless struggle. The triumphant message is clear; a new
German Berlin has arisen from the blood and tears shed by the likes of Horst Wessels.

187 **Kampf um Berlin: der Anfang.** (Struggle for Berlin: the beginning.)
Joseph Goebbels. Munich: Eher, 1934. 285p.
'The struggle for the capital city always represents a particular chapter in the history of revolutionary movements' (p. 11). This is how Goebbels begins his account of the struggle to conquer Berlin for the Nazis, responsibility for which had been accorded to him by Hitler. According to Goebbels, this struggle has lasted five years so far (the account ends in 1927, even though it was only published seven years later) and must be continued until the movement has achieved its goal. The book also contains photographs and drawings.

188 **The last Jews in Berlin.**
Leonard Gross. London: Sidgwick & Jackson, 1983. 349p.
When Hitler took power in January 1933, there were 160,000 Jews living in Berlin. By 1943 only a few thousand were still alive but existing 'underground' to avoid detection. Exactly how many were still alive at the end of the war is a matter of conjecture, estimates varying between a few hundred and several thousand. Using interviews with eighteen Jewish survivors which his colleague Eric Lasher had taped in Berlin in 1967, the journalist Leonard Gross selected 'several representative stories' involving ten survivors and, after checking them and further developing them with the survivors themselves, set them down in this book. A riveting read. See also Heinz R. Kuehn's autobiography, *Mixed blessings. An almost ordinary life in Hitler's Germany* (Athens, Georgia; London: University of Georgia Press, 1988. 206p.), The author, a half-Jew, describes how he lived through the Hitler years unscathed before emigrating to the United States in 1951. This book was also published by Simon & Schuster (New York, 1982. 349p.).

189 **The road to New York: the emigration of Berlin journalists, 1933-1945.**
Michael Groth. Munich, FRG: Minerva, 1984. 386p. bibliog.
This informative study of the many Berlin journalists who emigrated to the United States during the Third Reich was originally written as a doctoral dissertation for the University of Iowa.

190 **Bomber offensive.**
Sir Arthur Harris. London: Collins, 1947. 288p. index.
Harris, who was appointed Commander-in-Chief of Bomber Command on 23 February 1942, presents a detailed account of the controversial British bombing campaign against Germany and in particular Berlin which was conducted during the final years of the Second World War, costing the lives of many German civilians. See also D. Saward, *Bomber Harris*. London: Cassell, 1984.

191 **Hitler's Berlin: the Speer plans for reshaping the central city.**
Stephen D. Helmer. Ann Arbor, Michigan: UMI Research Press, 1985. 336p. bibliog. (Architecture and Urban Design, 14).
This is a scholarly analysis of the megalomaniac plans for the redesigning of the centre of Berlin which were produced by Speer at Hitler's request.

192 **Failure of a mission, Berlin 1937-1939.**
Sir Nevile Henderson. London: Hodder & Stoughton, 1940. 318p.
As British Ambassador in Berlin from April 1937 until the outbreak of the Second World War Sir Nevile Henderson strove in vain to preserve an honourable peace with

History. The Third Reich and the Second World War (1933-45)

Nazi Germany. That his mission ended in tragic failure he attributes to 'the fanatical megalomania and blind self-confidence of a single individual, and of a small clique of his self-interested followers'. His personal account of his time in Berlin, and particularly his descriptions of his encounters with the Nazi leadership, afford valuable insights into the situation in the capital as Germany moved inexorably towards war. The texts of important communications between the German and British governments are included (in English) as appendices (p. 299-318).

193   **Berlin alert: the memoirs and reports of Truman Smith.**
      Edited and with an introduction by Robert Hessen, foreword by
      General A. C. Wedemeyer.   Stanford, California: Hoover Institution
      Press, 1984. 172p. (Hoover Press Publication 289).
Truman Smith (1893-1970) was senior American military attaché in Berlin between August 1935 and April 1939, with particular responsibility for reporting on the growth of the German army, including the development of new weapons and new battle tactics. With the help of Charles Lindbergh he also drew attention to the rapid expansion of Germany's air power, although critics saw this as evidence that Lindbergh and Smith were Nazi sympathisers anxious to exaggerate the size of the German air force in order to demoralise the USA. Smith nevertheless continued to enjoy the confidence of General George C. Marshall. This collection of his papers includes a long section on his controversial air intelligence activities in Berlin in the four years before the beginning of the Second World War (p. 75-166).

194   **Blood and honour.**
      Reinhold Kerstan.   Tring, England: Lion Publishing, 1983. 170p.
      (A Lion Paperback).
Kerstan, the son of a pastor, became a member of the Hitler youth in Berlin after arriving there in 1937 when his father was appointed to serve a church in the district of Neukölln: 'I arrived in the throbbing capital of the Third Reich wide-eyed and alive to the marching music. Here in the next few years the seeds of Aryan superiority and militarism took root in my young heart, side by side with the gospel of peace and love' (p. 19-20). His narrative shows how he succumbed to the appeal of the National Socialists but was ultimately rescued by his upbringing in the Christian faith.

195   **Berliner Alltag im Dritten Reich.** (Daily life in Berlin during the Third
      Reich.)
      Gerhard Kiersch, Rainer Klaus, Wolfgang Kramer, Elisabeth
      Reichhardt-Kiersch.   Düsseldorf, FRG: Droste, 1981. 180p. bibliog.
A collection of 251 photographs, linked by an informative text, tells the story of National Socialism in Berlin from the time Hitler sent Goebbels there as Gauleiter in 1926 until 1945, with a final chapter devoted to attempts in the post-war period to deal with the Nazi heritage. The book also contains a useful chronological table of important events between 1926 and 1945.

196   **The Russians and Berlin, 1945.**
      Erich Kuby, translated from the German by Arnold J. Pomerans.
      New York; Hill & Wang; London: Heinemann, 1968. 372p. bibliog.
Making full use of eye-witness accounts and unpublished diaries, Kuby describes the Soviet advance on Berlin in 1945, the capture of the city, and the setting up of a Soviet

54

administration. His account was originally written as a series of articles which appeared in the West German news magazine *Der Spiegel* between 5 May and 9 June 1965, but these were considerably expanded for publication in book form. Kuby admits that he was still much too close to the events to have been able to say anything like the last word on them but insists that he 'made use only of those facts that have been satisfactorily proven'. The book includes numerous photographs, an index, maps and diagrams.

197 **Dimitroff's letters from prison.**
Compiled with explanatory notes by Alfred Kurella, translated by Dona Torr, Michael Davidson. London: Victor Gollancz Ltd. in association with Michael Lawrence Ltd, 1935. 160p.

Following the Reichstag fire on 27 February 1933, Dimitroff and two other Bulgarians were arrested by the Nazis on 9 March and put on trial in both Berlin and Leipzig where they were kept in prison. After their acquittal on 23 December 1933, Dimitroff spent a month in solitary confinement in the Gestapo's underground prison in Berlin before being allowed to depart for Moscow. The fifty-two letters published here cover the periods on remand, in court, after the acquittal, and in Moscow. There is an appendix, containing a letter from Dimitroff to the French writer Romain Rolland, extracts made by Dimitroff from the indictment (with his marginal notes), and two further entries from his notebooks.

198 **A mother fights Hitler.**
Irmgard Litten, translated from the German by Bernard Miall, foreword by His Grace the Archbishop of York (William Ebor), introduction by W. Arnold-Forster. London: George Allen & Unwin, 1940. 286p.

Irmgard Litten's moving account of the imprisonment and murder by the Nazis of her son, the prominent left-wing Berlin lawyer Hans Litten. The latter had called Hitler as a witness in a trial concerned with Nazi violence in the streets and had considerably embarrassed him during two hours of cross-examination. As Arnold-Forster notes, 'Hitler never forgave or forgot that ordeal'. After the Reichstag fire, Litten was one of the well-known opponents of Nazism who were quickly rounded up. He was imprisoned in Spandau without trial, charge, or sentence. Despite efforts in England to obtain his release, he was moved from camp to camp and tortured brutally. He died in Dachau in 1938, allegedly by hanging himself. In his short foreword the then Archbishop of York and later Archbishop of Canterbury, William Ebor, wrote: 'I hope this book will be widely read as a moving human record which illustrates the spirit of the Nazi tyranny'. The book was also published in the same year in Paris (Editions Nouvelles), New York (Alliance Book Corporation) Mexico City (Edicione Minerva) and Shangai (Kelley & Walsh). Like its London counterpart, the New York edition includes the (abbreviated) foreword by the Archbishop of York, the introduction (modified) by W. Arnold-Forster, and a full-page photograph of Irmgard Litten opposite the title-page. In addition it contains in its 325 pages an introduction and epilogue by Pierre van Paassen. The German edition, which had been seized by the Nazis on the eve of publication, did not appear until 1947 under the title *Eine Mutter kämpft* (Rudolstadt, GDR: Greifenverlag). The same publisher re-issued the book in 1985 under the title *Eine Mutter kämpft gegen Hitler*.

199   **La vie quotidienne à Berlin sous Hitler.** (Daily life in Berlin under
      Hitler.)
      Jean Marabini.   Paris: Hachette, 1985. 248p. bibliog. map.
A well-told history of the Nazi period by a French journalist. Despite its title,
however, this book is less about daily life than about the leading characters in a
German tragedy.

200   **1933.**
      Philip Metcalfe.   London, New York, Toronto, Sydney, Auckland:
      Bantam Press. 1989. 316p. bibliog.
Using letters, diaries, and published memoirs, Metcalfe sets out to describe Hitler's
seizure of power in 1933 and 1934 as seen through the experiences of five people – the
American Ambassaador in Berlin, William Dodd, and his daughter Martha; Hitler's
mercurial Chief of the Foreign Press, Putzi Hanfstaengel; a Jewish society reporter
working for the Ullstein newspaper empire, Bella Fromm; and the first head of the
Gestapo, the intelligent and ambitious Rudolf Diels. A portrait photograph of each of
them is included in the volume. Through his judicious choice of material and his ability
to deploy it so as to bring his characters to life in all their strengths and weaknesses,
Metcalfe succeeds in producing a lively and highly readable 'history of a revolution as
the participants lived it' (p. 7). He draws attention to a rich literature of eye-witness
accounts (listed in his excellent bibliography), including Martha Dodd's *Through
Embassy eyes* (1939), Bella Fromm's *Blood and banquets: a Berlin social diary* (1944),
and what he calls 'the most enthralling account of social ostracism and impending exile'
(p. 8), Eva Lips' *Savage symphony* (1938). Also revealing is *Ambassador Dodd's diary*
by William E. Dodd, Jr. and Martha Dodd (Gollancz: London, 1941). A paperback
version was issued by Bantam Books in 1989. In the same year the German translation
also appeared as *1933* (Stuttgart: Bonn Aktuell). One year later the volume was
published as a Black Swan Book (London: Transworld Publishers, 1990. 381p.
bibliog.).

201   **The Berlin raids: RAF Bomber Command winter 1943-44.**
      Martin Middlebrook.   Harmondsworth, England: Penguin, 1990.
      407p. bibliog. 19 maps.
This volume provides what the author believes is the first detailed account, in Britain
or Germany, of the nineteen major raids which Bomber Command made on Berlin
between August 1943 and March 1944. During the campaign, over 30,000 tons of
bombs were dropped on or near Berlin, killing 10,305 people and destroying over a
quarter of the city's built-up area. Despite the fact that 'no other Second World War
bombing campaign against a single target was pressed so hard, for so long and at such
cost as the attempt to destroy Berlin', Middlebrook supports those who (unlike Sir
Arthur 'Bomber' Harris himself) regard the raids as too costly in relation to the results
achieved: 'The Luftwaffe hurt Bomber Command more than Bomber Command hurt
Berlin'. The technical details of the raids are fleshed out and enlivened by extracts
from accounts of their experiences by some of the airmen involved on both sides.
Detailed appendices provide statistical and other information on the squadrons which
took part in the raids. Twenty-nine black-and-white photographs are also included.

202   **The Berlin bunker: the history of the Reich Chancellery group.**
James P. O'Donnell.   London: Arrow Books, 1979. 413p.

James P. O'Donnell, who as *Newsweek* correspondent was able to enter Hitler's Berlin bunker on the very day – 4 July 1945 – that American and British troops moved into the vanquished German capital, describes his book as 'a reconstruction' of the Führer's final weeks in his catacomb fifty-five feet below ground level, as experienced through 'the eyes, ears and memories' of those who were closest to him at that time and whom the author was able to interview in the 1970s. O'Donnell acknowledges his debt to Hugh Trevor-Roper's classic study *The last days of Hitler* (1947) (q.v.), with which he differs only in matters of detail. He defines this edition of his absorbing work as 'the definitive one, containing corrections I was unable to make in the American version' (published as *The Bunker. The history of the Reich Chancellery group.* Boston, Massachusetts: Houghton Mifflin, 1979. 399p. index.). The book includes twenty-six photographs and two illustrations and was also published in London by Dent in 1979.

203   **The fall of Berlin.**
Anthony Read, David Fisher.   London: Hutchinson, 1992. 513p. bibliog.

This detailed and well-written account of the final battle for Berlin at the end of the Second World War starts with the Olympic games which took place in Berlin in 1936. It includes five maps and eight pages of photographs.

204   **The last battle.**
Cornelius Ryan.   New York: Simon & Schuster, 1966. 573p. bibiliog.

The last battle of the Second World War was that for Berlin, the capital of the Nazis' much-vaunted Thousand Year Reich. It began on what the western allies called A-Day – the 16th of April 1945. Two weeks later Hitler was dead in his bunker, and after a further week the war was at last over. Cornelius Ryan's account of the battle and the events which led up to it sees itself not as a military report but as 'the story of ordinary people, both soldiers and civilians, who were caught up in the despair, frustration, terror and rape of the defeat and the victory' (p. 9). Over two thousand people – Americans, British, Russian, German, French, Danish, Dutch, and Swedish – contributed their recollections and their views to the writing of the book. The names and personal details of over 700 people who were contacted over a three-year period beginning in 1962 are included on p. 521-40. Ryan's interviews with key participants such as Eisenhower, Bradley, Montgomery, Koniev, Rokossovskii, and Heinrici enriches the narrative with a wealth of factual detail and insight. A riveting and informative read, the volume also includes an index, maps, photographs, and a plan of Hitler's bunker in Berlin (p. 424-25).

205   **The last thirty days: the war diary of the Wehrmacht high command
from April to May 1945.**
Joachim Schultz-Naumann, translated from the German by D. C.
Smith, introduction by Walter Hubatsch.   Lanham, Mayland:
University Press of America, 1989. 224p. bibliog.

Schultz-Naumann was the officer entrusted with keeping the official diary of the Wehrmacht during the final phases of the war in northern Germany. His account has an immediacy which makes it a valuable document of the times. It was first published in 1951 under the title *Die letzten dreißig Tage. Aus dem Kriegstagebuch des OKW* (Edited by Jürgen Thorwald. Stuttgart, FRG: Steingrüben). For a later edition, see *Die letzten dreißig Tage. Das Kriegstagebuch des OKW April bis Mai 1945. Die Schlacht um Berlin. Dokumente: Bilder und Urkunden* (introduction by Walter Hubatsch. Munich, FRG: Universitas, 1980. 248p. bibliog.).

206 **Wilfrid Israel: German Jewry's secret ambassador.**
Naomi Shepherd. London: Weidenfeld & Nicolson, 1984. 291p. bibliog.

Wilfrid Israel was the model for Bernhard Landauer, a character in Christopher Isherwood's novel *Goodbye to Berlin*. Based on the impression he had gained of Israel in Berlin, Isherwood portrayed him as a young Jewish businessman who is indifferent to Nazi threats – an injustice he later tried to correct. Israel was in fact a courageous man who helped the Jewish Agency in its attempts to rescue Jews under threat from fascism. This was to cost him his life in June 1943, when the unarmed plane on which he was flying from Lisbon to Bristol following a relief mission to refugee camps in Spain and Portugal was shot down over the Bay of Biscay by a Luftwaffe fighter patrol. Shepherd's book provides the first full, balanced account of the life of this in many respects enigmatic and reticent man.

207 **Berlin diary: the journal of a foreign correspondent, 1934-1941.**
William L. Shirer   New York: Knopf; London: Hamish Hamilton, 1941. 491p. Also London: Sphere, 1970. 493p. (A Sphere Paperback).

William Shirer was a distinguished Berlin correspondent for CBS from 1934 until December 1940. This book is made up of the diaries he kept at the time, excluding some notes that were lost and others which he deliberately burned for fear of detection. Some parts were committed to memory for the same reason and added later (Shirer is aware of the pitfalls of such a method), while some names were disguised in order to leave no clues for the Gestapo. After Shirer left his post, his successor from the end of 1940 until November 1941, Harry W. Flannery, continued the story in his book *Assignment to Berlin* (Michael Joseph: London, 1942. 310p.). After the end of the war Shirer returned to Berlin, remaining there until 1947. The record of what he observed at that time can be found in his *End of a Berlin diary* (New York: Popular Library, 1947. 351p. New York: Knopf; London: Hamish Hamilton, 1947. 369p.). These are invaluable documents from a particularly dark period in Berlin's history.

208 **Battlefield Berlin: siege, surrender and occupation.**
Peter Slowe, Richard Woods.   London: Robert Hale, 1988. 221p. bibliog.

This book uses diaries and personal records from a wide variety of English, French, German and Russian sources in order to paint a picture of Berlin during the final stages of Nazi rule and the first period of Communist and Western control which immediately followed. The sources ranges from Goebbels to soldiers of the Red Army and Jews hiding in Berlin. There are numerous photographs and diagrams as well as an index and an appendix.

209 **While Berlin burns: the diaries of Hans-Georg von Studnitz 1943-45.**
Hans-Georg von Studnitz, translated from the German by R. H.
Stevens. London: Weidenfeld & Nicolson, 1964. 290p.

Apart from one short break von Studnitz served in the information and press sections
of the German Foreign Ministry throughout the entire duration of the war. He reports
that his motives for publishing his diaries were twofold; firstly, few other people in his
situation were probably able to keep a diary, secondly, any assessment of the Nazi era
should not rely on official documents alone. Unfortunately, the jottings begin only in
1943, with the fall of Stalingrad. It is nevertheless a compelling read.

210 **The last days of Hitler.**
Hugh Trevor-Roper. London: Macmillan, 1978. 360p.; London:
Papermac, 1987. 288p.

In the months immediately following the end of the Second World War the
circumstances surrounding the death or disappearance of Adolf Hitler became the
source of much controversy. Claims that he had perished in Berlin during the final days
of the war competed with allegations that he had made a successful escape to one
refuge or another in various parts of Germany or the rest of the world. The Soviets,
who had been the first of the allies to enter Berlin and were therefore in the best
position to establish the facts, seemed unwilling or unable to do so and instead put
forward a variety of mutually contradictory explanations which only deepened the
mystery. In September 1945, therefore, British Intelligence apppointed Hugh Trevor-
Roper to investigate all the available evidence and to establish, if possible, the full
truth. His conclusion, originally presented in his report of 1st November 1945 and
further developed the following summer in what has become this classic study, is that
Hitler did die in Berlin on 30th April 1945 (as stated by Goebbels) and that there was
no reliable evidence to support any other explanation of his disappearance.

211 **The Berlin diaries of Marie 'Missie' Vassiltchikov.**
Marie Vassiltchikov, foreword by George Vassiltchikov. London:
Chatto & Windus, 1985. 324p.; London: Methuen, 1987. 324p.

Born in St. Petersburg in 1917 as the fourth of the five children of Prince and Princess
Illarion Vassiltchikov, the author of these fascinating diaries grew up in Germany,
France, and Lithuania and lived after the war in France, Spain, and England, dying of
leukemia in London in 1978. In January 1940 she and her sister Tatiana went to Berlin
in search of work (for stateless persons, this was not easy to find outside of Italy and
Germany). She became involved there with the anti-Nazi resisters involved in 'the 20th
July Plot', her close account of which is described in the foreword as 'the only known
eyewitness diary account in existence'. The version of her diaries published here was
completed, with minor changes to the original, only weeks before the author's death.
Parts of the diaries covering 1941, 1942, and 1943 are missing – 'destroyed deliberately,
lost, or beyond present reach', as the foreword rather mysteriously declares. Written in
English, the diaries were first published in part in *The Sunday Telegraph*. The book
includes an index, a glossary, maps, and twelve pages of photographs. American
editions of this work were published by Knopf (New York, 1987) and Vintage Books
(New York, 1988).

212 **Hausfrau at war: a German woman's account of life in Hitler's Reich.**
Else Wendel, in collaboration with Eileen Winncroft.   London:
Odhams Press, 1957. 255p.

The story of a young woman in Berlin from 1939 until the blockade of 1948/49. Although not a member of the National Socialist Party, she did work in the head office of the Labour Front. Much of the narrative is very personal in nature, focusing on the author's divorce, remarriage to 'the ideal man', and struggle to keep her children. Nevertheless, her final paragraph expresses the somewhat unconvincing ambition that her story should have wider significance: 'I have told the story of Berlin and exposed my own tragedy in doing so. All I hope is that it will help in some small way to a better understanding between Mr. and Mrs. Schmitt on the one side and Mr. and Mrs. Smith on the other' (p. 255).

The Post-War period (1945-)

General

213 **West Berlin: yesterday and today.**
Pyotr Abrasimov.   Dresden, GDR: Zeit im Bild, 1981. 165p. bibliog.
illus.

Originally published in Russian (Moscow, 1980), Abrasimov's book was revised and enlarged in this English translation (versions in German and French were also published). It represents the official Soviet account, under the name of the country's then Ambassador to the GDR (since 1962), of the 'diplomatic efforts made by the Soviet Union to deal with the West Berlin situation and to bring about the signing of the Quadripartite Agreement and its subsequent implementation' (p. 10). The text of the agreement is included in a section of documents (p. 153-165). While pledging himself to unconditional fulfilment of the agreement in the interests of detente and co-operation, Abrasimov ends with a chilling warning to those in the West, especially the Federal Republic, who might be tempted to infringe the rights of the Soviet Union and the GDR: '. . .the countries of the socialist community have ample means at their disposal to deal with these or any other illicit and aggressive intentions' (p. 148).

214 **Winds of history: the German years of Lucius DuBignon Clay.**
John H. Backer, foreword by John J. McCloy, epilogue by Don D.
Humphrey.   New York; Cincinnati, Ohio; Toronto, London;
Melbourne, Australia: Van Nostrand Reinhold Company, 1983. 323p.
bibliog.

Backer's aim is to show that the common perception of General Clay as a leading Cold War warrior whose greatest accomplishment was the Berlin airlift fails to do justice to his achievements as a leader with 'a rare sense of history and an almost prophetic political vision' who became 'the architect of a democratic West German republic' (p. 2).

215 Berlin days.
George Clare.   London: Macmillan, 1989. 230p. bibliog.
Born a second-generation Viennese Jew, George Clare emigrated to Britain at the approach of the Second World War. This amusing volume gives an account of his two years (1946-47) in Berlin as an interpreter with the Control Commission for Germany. A paperback edition has appeared under the title *Berlin days 1946-47* (London: Pan Books, 1990. 230p. bibliog.).

216 Berlin and the future of eastern Europe.
Edited by David S. Collier, Kurt Glaser.   Chicago: Henry Regnery, 1963. 251p. bibliog. (Foundation for Foreign Affairs Series, No. 7).
The twelve chapters of this book are based on papers delivered at an international conference held in Chicago in 1962. The conference is described by the editors as the first such meeting held since the Second World War at which east European problems were discussed by specialists of Polish, Czech, German, French and other European, as well as American, origins.

217 Reichstrümmerstadt: Leben in Berlin 1945-1961. (The rubble city of the Reich: life in Berlin 1945-1961.)
Sylvia Conradt, Kirsten Heckmann-Janz.   Darmstadt, FRG; Neuwied, FRG: Luchterhand, 1987. 222p. bibliog.
Contains the story of life in post-war Berlin as reflected in documents and over fifty photographs selected by the authors, who provide linking texts. The result is a highly readable chronicle which successfully evokes something of the spirit of the times.

218 The division of Berlin.
John Dudman.   Hove, England: Wayland, 1987. 76p. bibliog.
A brief, easy-to-read introduction to the division of Berlin until 1987. Like so many other commentators, however, the author regards the question of whether Germany and Berlin will ever be reunited as 'academic'. A chronology and glossary are also included along with numerous photographs. An American edition was published by Rourke Enterprises (Vero Beach, Florida, 1989).

219 Berlin – Hauptstadtanspruch und Westintegration. (Berlin – its claim to be capital, and integration in the West.)
Jürgen Fijalkowski, Peter Hauck, Axel Holst, Gerd-Heinrich Kemper, Alf Mintzel.   Cologne, Opladen, GDR: Westdeutscher Verlag, 1967. 353p. bibliog. (Schriften des Instituts für Politische Wissenschaft, vol. 20).
This scholarly volume deals authoritatively with three specific aspects of West Berlin's history in the first twenty years of the post-war era: the development of its political parties and trades unions; the question of West Berlin's theoretical status in law and the practical fact of its integration into the legal system of the Federal Republic; and the problems faced by West Berlin in adapting to the economic and social order in West Germany. Particular attention is paid to the immediate post-War years.

220 **Berlin between two worlds.**
Edited by Ronald A. Francisco, Richard L. Merritt, foreword by
Shepard Stone. Boulder, Colorado; London: Westview Press, 1986.
184p. bibliog.

This collection of ten essays by a team of American, West German and British scholars
offers a variety of perspectives on the status, role and problems of divided Berlin
within a divided Germany. Like most Western commentators in the mid-1980s, the
authors share the belief that there is little prospect of the division of the city being
overcome and that, as Merritt notes in the final lines of the book, 'In the place of
community, estrangement is growing' (p. 175).

221 **Berlin betrayal.**
Willi Frischauer. New York: Belmont Books, 1961. 221p. bibliog.

In 1950 Dr. Otto John became West Germany's first President of the Office for the
protection of the Constitution. Four years later, on 20 July 1954, he crossed over to
East Berlin and became a mouthpiece for East German propaganda directed
particularly against the alleged revival of Nazism in the Federal Republic. Since John
had an honourable history as a member of the German resistance against Hitler, being
directly involved in the attempt on Hitler's life on 20 July 1944 exactly ten years to the
day before his unexpected disappearance, and had subsequently taken refuge in
England where he worked under Sefton Delmer in the Special Operations Directorate
of the Psychological Warfare Executive, his move caused a sensation. Whether John –
described by Frischauer as 'freedom fighter, intelligence chief, symbol of a divided
Germany, a tragic Don Quixote of the Cold War' – deliberately defected or was simply
abducted could not be satisfactorily explained, not even after his dramatic escape back
to West Berlin in December 1955 and the subsequent trial at which he was condemned
to four years in prison.

222 **Documents on Berlin 1943-1963.**
Edited by Wolfgang Heidelmeyer, Günter Hindrichs. Munich, FRG:
Oldenbourg Verlag, 1963. 373p. bibliog. (Forschungsinstitut der
deutschen Gesellschaft für auswärtige Politik. Dokumente und Berichte
Band 22 – Englische Ausgabe).

This collection of 211 documents is the second revised and enlarged edition, in English,
of *Documents on the status of Berlin* edited by O. M. von der Gablentz (1958). It
includes a fold-out map of divided Berlin and of the post-War zones of occupation in
Germany.

223 **The future of Berlin.**
Edited by Martin J. Hillenbrand. Montclair, New Jersey: Allenheld,
Osmun Publishers, 1980. 314p. bibliog. (An Atlantic Institute for
International Affairs Research Volume).

This volume sets out to meet the need for an 'in-depth, broad-gauged, multidis-
ciplinary study that makes a realistic assessment of the city's present condition'. It does
so against the background of what the editor (a former US Ambassador to West
Germany) sees as increasing doubts about West Berlin's viability given the gradual
replacement in positions of influence of those with direct experience of Berlin's recent
history by a younger generation of policy-makers 'for many of whom the fate of the

city is increasingly removed from immediate concerns'. The six contributors to this book take a generally positive view of West Berlin's future possibilities. They pay particular attention to political factors, the legal background, urbanological perspectives (including housing, demographic trends, the presence of a large group of foreign migrants, schools, health, the drugs problem, unemployment), economic perspectives, the importance of Berlin as a centre of research, and the cultural scene, thus allowing the editor to conclude that West Berlin has the potential to become the 'model of a creative modern city'.

224 **Berlin command.**
Frank D. Howley.   New York: G. P. Putnam's Sons, 1950. 276p.

Brigadier General Frank Howley was commandant of the American sector of Berlin when the Soviet air blockade of the city took place. He makes no secret of his contempt for the Soviets – 'Communist rats who walked like bears', as he puts it in his foreword – and describes the Kremlin's decision to impose the blockade as 'the most barbarous in history since Ghengis Khan reduced conquered cities to pyramids of skulls' (p. 3). Beyond the rhetoric, however, this is a revealing account of Howley's four years in Berlin from 1945 to 1949, during which he was at the heart of the city's many crises and its struggle to recover from the War.

225 **Berlin 1945-1986: Geschichte der Hauptstadt der DDR.**
(Berlin 1945-1986: history of the capital of the GDR.)
Gerhard Keiderling.   Berlin (East): Dietz, 1987. 903p. bibliog. map.

A history of (East) Berlin written from the perspective of the SED (the ruling Socialist Unity Party of the GDR). On the eve of its 750th anniversary celebrations the capital of the GDR is presented as a dynamic and forward-looking city which 'reflects the achievements and ideals of the socialist nation of the GDR' (p. 860). Over one hundred photographs are also included.

226 **Berlin vom Brennpunkt der Teilung zur Brücke der Einheit.**
(Berlin from focal point of division to bridge of unity.)
Edited by Gerd Langguth.   Cologne: Verlag Wissenschaft und Politik, 1990. 504p. bibliog.

Originally scheduled to appear in autumn 1989, this fascinating collection of essays was held up for a further year in order both to allow the contributors time to react to and reflect on the implications of the collapse of the GDR and of the Warsaw Pact, and also to offer authors from the GDR the opportunity to add their views to the rich mix of ideas contained in the volume. The result is a work which, at an important turning-point in history, attempts to assess the historical, political, economic, and cultural role of Berlin in Germany, in Europe, and in the world. One section is dedicated to the views of eight former mayors of Berlin, including Willy Brandt and Richard von Weizsäcker. Another consists of contributions by representatives of the allied powers in Berlin – Sir Christopher Audland (UK), Jonathan Dean (USA) Henri Froment-Meurice (France), Walenti Koptelzew and Dmitri Tultschinski (USSR) – while the final section brings together the very different voices of authors from East and West Germany on the subject of Berlin in the 1990s. An informative appendix brings together essential statistics relating to both parts of Berlin.

227 **Berlin before the Wall: a foreign student's diary with sketches.**
Hsi-Huey Liang. New York, London: Routledge, 1990. 258p.

Liang spent the academic year 1953-54 as a student in West Berlin. While there, he kept diaries without any intention of publishing them. German unification gave them some significance as a record of what the author saw and thought at the height of the Cold War in Berlin, hence the decision to publish.

228 **Wartime origins of the Berlin dilemma.**
Daniel J. Nelson, foreword by William R. T. Fox. University, Alabama: University of Alabama Press, 1978. 219p. bibliog.

Nelson's book offers a careful account of the wartime negotiations among the four victorious allies which gave rise to Berlin's complicated post-war situation as a divided city within a divided country. Whilst warning against the too hasty judgment that this situation was the result of disastrous Western diplomacy and pointing to what he sees as West Berlin's success as 'an oasis of Western civilization and culture deep within the territory of the repressive East German régime' (p. 156), Nelson nevertheless concludes that the European Advisory Commission, which he describes as 'certainly one of the most useful and most extraordinary bodies in the history of allied wartime diplomacy' (p. 170), failed to secure for Berlin a properly viable set of arrangements for the post-war period. The volume includes three maps and twelve annexes containing documents in English.

229 **Kultur, Pajoks und CARE-Pakete: eine Berliner Chronik 1945-1949.**
(Culture, special rations, and CARE-packets: a Berlin chronicle 1945-49.)
Winfried Ranke, Carola Jüllig, Jürgen Reiche, Dieter Vorsteher, edited by the Verein der Freunde und Förderer des Berlin Museums in Zusammenarbeit mit dem Berlin Museum, foreword by Jürgen Bostelmann, Rolf Bothe. Berlin: NiSHEN, 1990. 286p. bibliog.

The idea for this attractively produced book grew out of an exhibition, organized jointly by the Berlin Museum and the Centre for Industrial Culture in Nuremberg, on the struggle by German cities to recover from the destruction of war after 1945. It presents a chronologically-arranged overview of the immediate post-war years in Berlin and in particular of the gradual re-emergence of the city as a cultural metropolis. An excellent selection of photographs and of quotations from a variety of sources is accompanied by a lively and highly informative text. It is compelling reading.

230 **Modelling and managing international conflicts: the Berlin crises.**
Raymond Tanter. Beverley Hills, California; London: Sage, 1974. 272p. bibliog. (Sage Library of Social Research, vol. 6).

The purpose of this book is to compare systematically what the author calls 'East-West interactions over Berlin for 1948-1949 and 1961' (p. 12). Pointing to other scholars who have adopted a similar approach, Tanter aims to make his analyses even more systematic than anything previously attempted by using sophisticated quantitative data. He attempts to provide a link between strategic and comparative approaches on the one hand and quantitative techniques on the other. Not a book for the general reader but one which contributes usefully to an investigation of the Berlin crises as examples of conflict management.

231 **Documents on Germany 1944-1985.**
United States Department of State Historical Office. Washington, DC:
US Department of State, Office of the Historian, Bureau of Public
Affairs, 1985. 4th expanded ed. 1429p. bibliog. (Department of State
Publication 9446).

This volume presents an authoritative documentary record of United States foreign
policy towards Germany since the final stages of the Second World War. It includes the
most important agreements, exchanges, statements, speeches, and other public papers,
with special attention being paid to the situation in Berlin.

232 **Berlin und die deutsche Frage.** (Berlin and the German question.)
Udo Wetzlaugk. Cologne: Verlag Wissenschaft und Politik, 1985.
272p. bibliog. (Bibliothek Wissenschaft und Politik Band 36).

This searching investigation of the link between Berlin's status and the German
question was written at a time when the balance of power in Europe between East and
West seemed basically stable and lasting. In the author's view, the situation of divided
Berlin demonstrates with unique clarity the importance of peaceful negotiation and
political flexibility, which, he says, may not bring about the reunification of Germany
at one fell swoop but will continue to make the border more and more porous. The
book is therefore an important example of mainstream West German thinking on
Berlin in the mid-1980s, when any suggestion that the East would collapse a few years
later would have seemed far-fetched indeed.

The Airlift (1948-49)

233 **Decision in Germany.**
Lucius D. Clay. Melbourne, Australia; London, Toronto:
Heinemann; Westport, Connecticut: Greenwood Press, 1950. 522p.
bibliog.

This volume, which includes photographs and a chronological table for 1945-49,
recounts the story of the Berlin Airlift from the point of view of General Clay (q.v.),
the man most closely identified with its success. A reprint of the book is still available.

234 **Bridge across the sky: the Berlin Blockade and Airlift 1948-1949.**
Richard Collier. London: Macmillan; New York: McGraw Hill, 1978.
239p. map. bibliog.

The dramatic story of the Soviet blockade of Berlin between June 1948 and May 1949
is here retold in the best tradition of 'fly-on-the-wall' journalism. Collier's highly
readable narrative benefits from his interviews with many of the pilots, officials, and
others who participated in the successful struggle to break the blockade. Eight pages of
photographs, a chronology of events, a map, and an index are also included.

235 **The Berlin Blockade: a study in Cold War politics.**
W. Phillips Davison. Princeton, New Jersey: Princeton University
Press, 1958. 423p. bibliog.; New York: Arno Press, 1980. 423p. bibliog.

Written as part of a research programme undertaken for the US Air Force by the Rand
Corporation, this impressive study highlights the importance of the Berlin Blockade as
an opportunity to observe the operation of Western and Soviet diplomacy, the reaction
of Berlin's population to severe physical and psychological stress, and the role played
by public opinion throughout the crisis. Davison sees the Soviets as pursuing ruthlessly
a clearly defined strategy in mounting the blockade, whereas Western policy was
essentially indecisive, ill-focused, and unplanned. Nevertheless, Western leaders
ultimately proved resourceful and flexible enough to reach necessary, if last-minute
decisions. Their fundamental decency contrasted favourably with Soviet insensitivity
and gained for them the trust of the Berlin population, allowing the West to emerge
victorious from the crisis. The Berliners are presented in Davison's account as a hardy
people prepared to fight vigorously for their liberty. The book includes four pages of
black-and-white photographs and two maps.

236 **Bridge in the sky.**
Frank Donovan. New York: D. McKay, 1968. 209p. bibliog.;
London: Hale, 1970. 209p. bibliog.

Donovan sees the Berlin Airlift as the first clear post-War indication that the Anglo-
Americans were determined to prevent the spread of Communism throughout Europe.
He makes it clear that, in his view, Soviet success in the blockade would have meant
precisely that. Donovan believes that it was a strategic political error that the Western
allies allowed the Soviets to take Berlin at the end of the Second World War. It was
therefore all the more imperative not to give in to the Soviets on this occasion.
Moreover, the obligation to save Berlin was not just political but, in Donovan's view,
had a powerful moral dimension: the duty to resist oppression. 'To bow to Communist
tyranny would have been to yield to the same weakness for which they [the Western
allies] had so recently condemned the Germans' (p. 199). The volume includes twenty
photographs and two sketch maps.

237 **Blockade: Berlin and the Cold War.**
Eric Morris. New York: Stein & Day, 1973. 278p. bibliog; London:
Hamish Hamilton, 1973. 278p. bibliog.

Morris deals with the history of Berlin from the great battle for the city at the end of
the Second World War until the signing of the Berlin (or Quadripartite) Agreements in
September 1971. He welcomes the latter as a significant contribution towards
overcoming the Cold War, as 'the closest Europe can ever expect to come to a peace
treaty to end the Second World War' (p. 244), and as the occasion for East Germany
at last to become a full participant in European politics. The volume contains twelve
pages of black-and-white photographs and five maps.

238 **The United States and the Berlin Blockade, 1948-49: a study in crisis decision-making.**
Avi Shlaim, foreword by Michael Brecher. Berkeley, California; Los Angeles, London: University of California Press, 1983. 463p. bibliog. (International Crisis Behavior Project).
Within the research design launched in 1975 by the International Crisis Behavior Project, Shlaim investigates the conclusions reached by American decision-makers as they confronted the political stresses produced by the Berlin Blockade. His assessment leads him to question the widely held view that 'high and protracted stress seriously and adversely affects decision processes and outcomes' (p. 422).

239 **The Berlin Blockade.**
Ann Tusa, John Tusa. London: Hodder & Stoughton, 1988. 445p. map. bibliog. (Published in the United States under the title *The Berlin airlift.* Boston, Massachusetts: Atheneum, 1988. 445p. map. bibliog.).
Packed with readable detail, this painstakingly-researched account of the Soviet blockade of West Berlin from spring 1948 until summer 1949 pays tribute to the heroism of allied airmen who, against the odds, kept the Western sectors of the city supplied with enough food and other resources (a phenomenal 2,325,808 tons in all) to keep body and soul together. The authors stress equally the resilience and epic fortitude of the Berliners themselves, qualities which, displayed in the face of the notable apathy and occasional hostility of their compatriots in the Western zones, 'won the admiration of the world' and 'transformed hatred and fear of Germans into respect and alliance' (p. 477). It is nevertheless a sobering thought that the success of the airlift probably owed at least as much to the miracle of an extraordinarily mild winter – 'sheer meteorological freak' (p. 391) – and to Soviet blunders and ineptitude as to the prodigious efforts of the Berliners and of the pilots intent on their rescue. The book also includes sixteen pages of plates and an index. A paperback version (excluding the plates) was published in 1989 by Coronet Books, a subsidiary of Hodder & Stoughton.

The Workers' Uprising (1953)

240 **Uprising in East Germany: 17 June 1953.**
Arnulf M. Baring, translated from the German by Gerald Onn, introduction by David Schoenbaum, foreword by Richard Loewenthal. Ithaca, New York; London: Cornell University Press, 1972. 194p. Reprint of 1965 edition.
Baring's account of the 1953 Uprising was published in German as *Der 17. Juni 1953* (Cologne, Berlin (West): Kiepenheuer & Witsch, 1965; 2nd edition Stuttgart, FRG: Deutsche Verlagsanstalt, 1983. 199p.). His analysis is basically as sound today as when it first appeared. He deals objectively with the events which preceded the uprising as well as describing the events themselves, coming to the conclusion that the circumstances which brought about the uprising certainly satisfied Lenin's definition of a revolutionary situation. Writing from the vantage-point of the mid-sixties, he believes that the West's passivity in the face of events in the East makes it unlikely that such a revolutionary situation will recur, particularly since the East German population

appears to have reached an accommodation with its leaders. The 1989 revolution may have disproved the latter point, but Baring's book retains its value for anyone interested in a balanced view of the events of June 1953.

241 The East German rising, 17th June 1953.

Stefan Brant (pseud. for Klaus Harpprecht), translated from the German by Charles Wheeler, foreword by John Hynd, M. P.

London: Thames & Hudson, 1955; New York: Praeger, 1957. 202p.

This is a well-informed and generally reliable account of the East German rising of 1953 which began when building workers on East Berlin's prestigious new Stalinallee went on strike in protest at the government's harsh economic policies. It is written from an explicitly anti-communist position which occasionally spills over into exaggeration, as when Rudolf Herrnstadt, the editor of *Neues Deutschland* and the victim of a purge shortly after the rising, is referred to as 'a Red Goebbels' (p. 171), or when it is said that it was the entire population of 18 million which struck against their political leaders: 'there was not a factory or a town in which the government's removal was not the cardinal demand' (p. 187). The author sees the rising as an undertaking of noble spontaneity which restored their dignity to all Germans and which failed precisely because it *was* spontaneous and therefore lacked the cool-headed strategy which might have outwitted the Communists. He argues that the early reunification of Germany has been made more likely by the rising, speaking of 'the Germany whose life began in the jubilation and the torment of June 17' and adding: 'The seventeenth of June sought a Germany which does not yet exist' (p. 199). Seen from this perspective, the process by which Germany achieved unification in 1990 began in 1953. The volume also includes ten black-and-white photographs and a map of East Germany showing the main centres of the rising. The original German version of the book was entitled *Der Aufstand: Vorgeschichte, Geschichte und Deutung des 17. Juni 1953* (Stuttgart: Steingrüben Verlag, 1954. 325p.).

242 The plebeians rehearse the uprising: a German tragedy.

Günter Grass, translated from the German by Ralph Manheim.

London: Secker & Warburg, 1967. 122p. bibliog.

Set in Berlin against the background of the events of 17 June 1953, Grass's play deals with the role of the intellectual in society and, more particularly, with the German tradition of the intellectual who avoids political involvement. The central character, known as the Boss, is clearly based on Bertolt Brecht. The book includes useful historical notes by Uta Gerhardt as well as an introductory text by Grass.

243 Five days in June: a novel.

Stefan Heym.   London: Hodder & Stoughton, 1977; Buffalo, New York: Prometheus Books, 1978. 352p.

Heym's powerful novel is based on the popular uprising which took place in East Berlin and East Germany in mid-June 1953. In Heym's view, the uprising was in part caused by the carefully orchestrated mischief of Western *agents provocateurs*, but it was equally certainly the result of gross political miscalculations by the ruling Communists in the East. Since this account deviates significantly from the version of events which East Germany's political élite favoured, the novel could not be published in the GDR until after the East German state had collapsed in 1989.

244   **Der 17. Juni.** (The 17th of June.)
       Curt Rieß.   Berlin (West): Ullstein, 1954. 260p. bibliog.
Rieß provides an eminently readable account of the Uprising which took place in East
Berlin and East Germany on 17 June 1953.

245   **17. Juni 1953: Arbeiteraufstand in der DDR.** (17th June 1953: workers'
       rising in the GDR.)
       Edited by Ilse Spittmann, Karl Wilhelm Fricke.   Cologne: Verlag
       Wissenschaft und Politik, 1982. 224p. bibliog. (Edition Deutschland
       Archiv).
Written three decades after the events of 17 June 1953 had taken place, this useful
volume was produced as an antidote to what Karl Wilhelm Fricke regarded as a signal
failure in both West and East Germany to recognize the full significance of the
Workers' Uprising. It has three principal sections: analyses of important aspects of the
rising, including an essay by Gerhard Wettig on Soviet policy towards Germany prior
to 17 June and a detailed analysis by Heinrich Mohr of the way in which GDR
literature from the 1950s to the 1970s dealt with such an ideologically sensitive topic; a
collection of reports and reflections by contemporaries; and a helpful selection of
documents. A chronological table of the main events and a selection of photographs
complete the volume.

246   **Rudolf Herrnstadt: das Herrnstadt-Dokument: das Politbüro der SED
       und die Geschichte des 17. Juni 1953.** (Rudolf Herrnstadt: the
       Herrnstadt document: the politburo of the Socialist Unity Party and the
       history of the 17th June 1953.)
       Edited by Nadja Stulz-Herrnstadt.   Reinbek, Germany: Rowohlt,
       1990. 288p. bibliog. (Rororo Aktuell 12837).
From 1950 to 1953 Rudolf Herrnstadt was Editor in Chief of *Neues Deutschland*, the
newspaper published in Berlin by the ruling Socialist Unity Party (SED). He was also a
candidate member of the GDR's politburo. Within the SED both he and Wilhelm
Zaisser were the most prominent critics of its Stalinist leader Walter Ulbricht. For a
brief spell before and after the workers' rising of 17th June 1953 they appeared to have
the majority of the politburo behind them, and Ulbricht's fall seemed likely. However,
the power struggle in Moscow following Stalin's death in March 1953 ultimately
allowed the wily Ulbricht to recover his position, and it was Herrnstadt and Zaisser
who were then removed from office and from the party. This document, edited by
Herrnstadt's daughter, gives an insider's view of the impact of the rising on the party
leadership in East Berlin. It was written in 1956 and provides what the editor describes
as 'the first and, up to now, only exact reconstruction' of events within the leadership
of party and state in 1953. In addition to the document itself and the editor's
informative introduction, the volume includes excerpts from a secret speech by
Ulbricht and from a letter which Herrnstadt addressed to the Deputy Foreign Minister
of the Soviet Union. There is also a section from Herrnstadt's memoirs, a biographical
note on Herrnstadt by his daughter, and an index.

The Wall (1961-89)

247 **The lost graffiti of Berlin: the writing on the Wall.**
Francesco Alacevich, Alessandro Alacevich, translated from the Italian
by Patricia Cavagnaro, introduction by Ruggero Guarini. Rome:
Gremese, 1991. 158p.

This volume of photographs captures some of the often surprisingly sophisticate
graffiti which covered parts of the Berlin Wall.

248 **We the people: the revolution of '89, witnessed in Warsaw, Budapest,
Berlin and Prague.**
Timothy Garton Ashe. London: Granta Books in association with
Penguin Books, 1990. 159p.

Timothy Garton Ashe enjoys a deserved reputation as one of the most perceptive and
knowledgeable commentators on the wave of change which swept across Europe in
1989. In this short book he devotes a particularly thoughtful chapter, entitled 'Berlin
Wall's end' (p. 61-77), to the fall of the Wall and its consequences. Written in January
1990, it captures with impressive immediacy the original euphoria which held the city
in its grip – that 'moment of emancipation and liberation, created by the people of East
Germany for the people of East Germany' (p. 77) – but notes, too, the rapid change of
mood to consternation and alarm. The book was also published in the USA under the
title *The magic lantern: the revolution of '89: witnessed in Warsaw, Budapest, Berlin
and Prague* (New York: Random House, 1990. 158p.).

249 **Every wall shall fall.**
Hellen Battle. Old Tappan, New Jersey: Hewitt House, 1969. 318p.

The story, in her own words, of an impressionable, naïve, but also wilful young
American girl who, while studying psychology and theology at West Berlin's Free
University in the mid-1960s, became involved in an unsuccessful attempt to help an
East German to escape across the Berlin Wall. Sentenced to four years' hard labour in
Bautzen prison, she was released after just over a year following the intervention of
Bertrand Russell. During her imprisonment, Hellen Battle came to believe in the
power of love as the means to achieve what she calls God's revolution throughout the
world.

250 **Berlin in the East-West struggle 1958-61.**
Glen D. Camp, Jr. New York: Facts on File, 1971. 252p. bibliog.

This volume is intended to fill the perceived need for 'a handy account in English that
offered both a sampling of the relevant documents and a completely objective
narrative of the events that would show how Berlin fared in the East-West struggle in
the period 1958-61' (p. 1). The text is correspondingly sober and factual in tone, with
no sign of Cold War rhetoric but, equally, no attempt at an explicit, reasoned
evaluation of the events outlined. A glossary of terms is also included.

251 **The ides of August: the Berlin Wall crisis.**
Curtis Cate. New York: M. Evans, 1978. 534p. bibliog.

A lively, well-informed, and combative account of the events leading to the
construction of the Berlin Wall. Cate concludes that, just as America's (in his view)

weak response to the 1948 blockade of Berlin had encouraged Stalin to launch the Korean War, so its 'mouselike reaction to the challenge of August 13 and the erection of Walter Ulbricht's wall was to lead to the Cuban missile crisis of October 1962' (p. 495). Cate's related charge that the British minister and deputy commandant in Berlin, Geoffrey McDermott, made no secret of his government's disapproval of General Lucius D. Clay's wish to adopt a more aggressive posture towards the Soviets over the Wall and that he even went so far as to assure the Russians that Clay's days in Berlin were numbered stands in curious contradiction with McDermott's own account (q.v.), in which he expresses surprise at the way in which Clay was treated by Washington for his views and actions. The volume includes a glossary, sixteen pages of photographs nine maps, and an index. An English edition entitled *The ides of August. The Berlin Wall crisis of 1961*, was published in London by Weidenfeld & Nicolson in 1978.

252 **Kennedy and the Berlin Wall crisis: a case study in US decision making.**
Honoré M. Catudal, foreword by Martin J. Hillenbrand. Berlin
(West): Berlin Verlag, 1980. 358p. bibliog.

Catudal's approach in this volume is what he refers to as the 'rational actor' model of decision-making analysis. His conclusion is that, contrary to what is often assumed by analysts of decision-making, rationality may well play a crucial role in how decisions are reached. Indeed, he describes John F. Kennedy's decision not to intervene in East Berlin after 13 August 1961 as 'one of the most clearly documented examples in modern times of an American Chief Executive rising above "bureaucratic inertia" to play an active and crucial role in the shaping of a sharply contested major foreign policy decision' (p. 11). What Kennedy and his advisors failed to consider properly, however, were the consequences of their decision, particularly for morale in Berlin and West Germany. Catudal's study exploits previously classified materials as well as the oral and written testimony of key participants. The book contains an index, photographs, and appendices (including a chronology of events for 1960-61). For an interesting analysis of the impact of the Wall on one small community in Berlin, see the same author's *Steinstücken. A study in Cold War politics* (Foreword by Lucius D. Clay. New York: Vantage Press, 1971. 165p. bibliog.).

253 **The Wall and how it fell.**
Edited by Götz von Coburg, foreword by Eberhard Diepgen. Berlin:
Press and Information Office of the Land of Berlin, 1990. 62p. bibliog.
(Dokumentation Berlin).

This booklet, published free of charge by Berlin's Press and Information Office, provides an informative introduction to the history of the Berlin Wall.

254 **Up against the Wall: the political and moral development of children in East and West Berlin.**
Thomas Andrew Davey. PhD thesis, Harvard University, Cambridge,
Massachusetts, 1984. (Available from Ann Arbor, Michigan: UMI
Dissertation Information Service, 1991, 302p. bibliog.).

This doctoral thesis, presented at Harvard University in 1984, investigates major factors which contributed to the development in children in East and West Berlin of feelings of loyalty towards or alienation from their nation. It relies on interviews with children, participation in their daily lives, thematic analysis of their drawings, and interviews with teachers and family members. The author is left at the end uncertain whether the children will, in time, come to regard not Germany but *West* or *East* Germany as the nation with which they identify.

255 **Berlin : the Wall is not forever.**
Eleanor Lansing Dulles, foreword by Konrad Adenauer. Chapel Hill, North Carolina: University of North Carolina Press, 1967. 245p. bibliog.

In her preface the author expresses her firm conviction that the Wall will fall within a reasonable period of time: 'Not at once, and perhaps not even at the same time, the Wall will come down and Germany will be reunited. The time and manner cannot be predicted'. The events of 1989 demonstrated that her confidence was justified, but it is clear from her book that she was worried in the mid-1960s by signs of an incipient 'gap of misunderstanding' (p. 213) between the United States and many young people in West Berlin and the Federal Republic. Her recommendation is therefore that American policymakers should intensify their dialogue with young Germans: 'Progress in this respect depends on a sensitive approach to the psychological problems of post-Hitler youth' (p. 213).

256 **Opfer der Mauer: die geheimen Protokolle des Todes.**
(Victims of the Wall: the secret protocols of death.)
Werner Filmer, Heribert Schwan. Munich: Bertelsmann, 1991. 431p. bibliog.

What the authors call 'simple realities' concerning the barbarity of the Berlin Wall are recorded in this book, using documents, statements, and interviews. These include previously unpublished daily reports by members of the People's Police (*Volkspolizei*) and the border guards. Of the many known cases of death at the Wall, four are chosen for particular investigation – those of Silvio Proksch, Michael Schmidt, Michael Bittner, and the last person to be shot while trying to escape, Chris Gueffroy. The names of over eighty guards who shot and killed would-be escapers are given here for the first time. In addition, one section is devoted to the deaths of two border guards. Against this background, it is hardly surprising that the authors clearly believe that Erich Honecker should be made to return from his refuge in the former Soviet Union (as he subsequently did) and face charges for his responsibility for so many murders.

257 **The Berlin Wall.**
Pierre Galante, with Jack Miller. London: Barker, 1965. 236p.

A journalistic account of the impact of the building of the Berlin Wall on 'the little people of the divided city' (p. 9) such as Harry Seidel, whose story is at the heart of the book. On 29 December 1962 Seidel was sentenced to penal servitude for life by the Supreme Court of the GDR for his part in organizing the attempted escape to the West of a number of East Germans, including members of his own family.

258 **The Berlin Wall.**
Norman Gelb. London: Michael Joseph, 1986. 298p. bibliog.

Norman Gelb was a correspondent in Berlin at the time the Wall was built in August 1961, and his book succeeds in capturing some of the drama of that key moment in post-War history. It also analyses the key events which led to and followed on from the erection of the Wall. The volume includes sixteen pages of plates, maps, and an index. The US edition is entitled *The Berlin Wall: Kennedy, Khruschev, and a showdown in the heart of Europe*, New York: Times Books, 1987; New York: Simon & Schuster, 1988. 321p. bibliog.

259 **The rise and fall of the Berlin Wall.**
R. G. Grant. Leicester, England: Magna Books, 1991. 160p.
R. G. Grant's excellent short history of the post-War division of Berlin and of Germany is accompanied here by a splendid selection of photographs.

260 **Die Berliner Mauer, Vorgeschichte Bau Folgen: Literaturbericht und Bibliographie zum 20. Jahrestag des 13. August 1961.** (The Berlin Wall, its pre-history, construction, and consequences: a report on the literature and a bibliography to mark the twentieth anniversary of 13th August 1961.)
Michael Haupt, foreword by Jürgen Rohwer, introduction by Willy Brandt. Munich: Bernard & Graefe, 1981. 230p. (Schriften der Bibliothek für Zeitgeschichte. Weltkriegsbücherei Stuttgart. Neue Folge der Bibliographien der Weltkriegsbücherei, vol. 21).
This is an exhaustive bibliography of items relating to the Berlin Wall which were known and accessible to the compiler for the period from August 1961 to December 1980. These include books, parts of books, journal articles, and newspaper articles. The first part of the bibliography is devoted to the Post-War period preceding the building of the Wall (p. 17-33). The volume concludes with a list of all periodicals consulted by the compiler (p. 212-19) and with a helpful index listing all the authors whose works are cited in the bibliography.

261 **Die Mauer spricht.** (The wall speaks.)
Text and selection of photographs by Rainer Hildebrandt. Berlin: Verlag am Checkpoint Charlie, 1990. 64p.
A collection of photographs which illustrate the changing face of the Wall through the successive phases of its existence. The accompanying text is in German and English. Another informative pamphlet on the Wall by the same author is entitled *It happened at the Wall*, Berlin: Haus am Checkpoint Charlie, 1990 (text in German, English, French, Italian, and Spanish).

262 **Memories of the Berlin Wall: history and the impact of critical life events.**
Erika M. Hoerning. *International Journal of Oral History*, vol. 8, no. 2, p. 95-111.
This article describes an attempt by sociologists to discover what happened to West Berliners who were directly affected by the building of the Berlin Wall. Beginning in 1983 a series of recorded interviews was conducted with thirty-nine men and women, all of whom had been born between 1903 and 1941 and had been either 'border commuters' (*Grenzgänger*) or 'border traders' at the time of the Wall's erection. This exercise in 'life-event studies' reveals that the long-term consequences which the building of the Wall exerted on particular biographies varied widely, depending not least on what Hoerning calls an individual's 'strategies for bibliographical action' and 'processes of evolutionary transformation'.

263 **Escape from Berlin.**
Anthony Kemp. London: Boxtree, 1987. 173p. bibliog.
Based on research originally undertaken for the Television South documentary film *Hanni sends her love*, this book tells the story of some of those who risked their liberty and even their lives trying to cross the Wall. Individual chapters are devoted to Wolfgang Fuchs, who masterminded over 500 escapes, and Wolf Quasner, a somewhat controversial entrepreneur among the escape organizers who, in the late 1970s, 'set out to provide an honest service for a reasonable fee' (p. 107). The volume includes thirty-six photographs, a map, and a diagram of frontier fortifications in divided Berlin.

264 **Berliner MauerKunst.** (Berlin WallArt).
Heinz J. Kuzdas, foreword by Walter Momper. Berlin: Elefanten Press, 1990. 84p.
Photographs of the paintings and graffiti on the Berlin Wall. The accompanying text, written by Michael Nungesser, is also provided in English, Spanish, and Japanese translation, as is the foreword by West Berlin's Lord Mayor, Walter Momper.

265 **Berlin: hostage for the West.**
John Mander. Harmondsworth: Penguin, 1962. 126p. (A Penguin Special); Westport, Connecticut: Greenwood Press, 1979. 124p.
Written six months after the Wall was erected, this book argues that if the West had removed it within twenty-four hours, they could have done so with impunity. This opportunity having been missed, the Wall should nevertheless be regarded as negotiable and the West should demand its removal. Even if that fails, every effort should be made to ensure West Berlin's security and economic viability while at the same time developing a positive political strategy towards the East with the aim of achieving reunification-in-freedom for Germany. Mander closes by quoting Lenin's words with approval: 'Whoever holds Berlin, holds Germany. Whoever holds Germany, holds Europe' (p. 124).

266 **Up against it: photographs of the Berlin Wall.**
Leland Rice, essay by Charles E. McLelland, foreword by Van Deren Coke. Albuquerque, New Mexico: University of New Mexico Press, 1991. 141p.
The photographs of the Berlin Wall which make up this volume were taken mainly in the 1980s.

267 **Living with the Wall: West Berlin, 1961-1985.**
Edited by Richard L. Merritt, Anna J. Merritt. Durham, North Carolina: Duke University Press, 1985. 242p. bibliog. (Duke Press Policy Studies).
Delivered in their original form at a conference organized by the Aspen Institute, Berlin, and the Science Centre, Berlin, in 1981, the papers in this volume explore the consequences of the building of the Wall for life in Berlin after 1961; the effects of the Quadripartite and Inter-German Agreements in the early 1970s; and the role of Berlin in its international context. Although the emphasis is clearly on the Western part of the city, East Berlin equally obviously plays a central part in the discussion, notably in Richard L. Merritt's useful consideration of 'interpersonal transactions across the Wall'

(p. 166-83). Other contributors are Klaus Schütz (West Berlin's mayor from 1967 to 1977), Jonathan Dean, Dieter Mahncke, Martin J. Hillenbrand, Wolfgang Watter (on West Berlin's economy), and Jürgen Engert.

268 **Die Mauer: vom Anfang und vom Ende eines deutschen Bauwerks.** (The Wall: on the beginning and end of a German construction.)

Jürgen Petschull. Hamburg: Gruner + Jahr, 1989. 2nd rev. ed. 288p.

This volume contains a superb collection of photographs which capture many of the most dramatic moments in the history of the Wall after its erection on 13 August 1961. Jürgen Petschull, a leading reporter with the magazine *Stern*, provides a jounalist's detailed account of events in Berlin between 10 August and 22 August, with a strong emphasis on 'human interest' stories – for example, that of Conrad Schumann, the first East German border guard who fled to the West and whose dramatic jump over a makeshift barbed wire barrier was captured in a memorable photograph by Klaus Lehnartz which appeared in newspapers across the world (reproduced here on p. 96-97). Separate chapters are devoted to 30 September 1989, when 6,000 GDR citizens took refuge on the territory of the West German Embassy in Prague until Foreign Minister Hans-Dietrich Genscher announced they were free to travel to the West, and to 9-10 November 1989, the night on which the GDR government at last succumbed to intense pressure and allowed freedom of travel across the Wall. A section of twenty-eight documents is also included (p. 214-75).

269 **August 1961: die Mauer von Berlin.** (13th August 1961: the Berlin Wall.)

Jürgen Rühle, Gunter Holzweißig. Cologne: Verlag Wissenschaft und Politik, 1981. 176p. bibliog. (Edition Deutschland Archiv).

This useful collection containing approximately a hundred documents, helpfully annotated by Gunter Holzweißig and set in their historical context by Jürgen Rühle's short introductory essay, covers the history of the Berlin Wall from Krushchev's famous ultimatum to the Western powers in 1958 to the attempt, in the Quadripartite Agreement of 1971, to come to terms with the division of the city. The volume includes statistical tables, diagrams, photographs, and a chronological table of events.

270 **The Berlin crisis 1958-1962.**

Jack M. Schick. Philadelphia: University of Pennsylvania Press, 1971. 266p. bibliog.

This book investigates the second Berlin crisis, which led directly to the building of the Berlin Wall. It is based on careful research and takes account of the views of the many experts interviewed by the author. Schick argues that 'Berlin crises are Moscow's way of opposing Bonn's policies: in 1958 it feared nuclear weapons acquisition'.

271 **Eine deutsche Geschichte: zwei Schwestern in Berlin – Bilder und Gespräche.** (A German story: two sisters in Berlin – pictures and conversations.)

Wolfgang Schwarze, Monika Schulz-Fieguth, Manfred Durniok. Berlin: Aufbau, 1990. 172p.

On 9 November 1990, exactly one year after the opening of the Berlin Wall, ZDF (Zweites Deutsches Fernsehen, one of Germany's most important television channels) broadcast a film by Gitta Nickel and Wolfgang Schwarze about the moving story of two sisters, Ursula Lesekrug and Waltraud Block, who grew up together in Berlin. There they experienced the war, the defeat of Germany, and the founding of the GDR. The sisters were separated in 1969 when Ursula and her two children were at last able to join her husband in West Berlin, their freedom having been bought by the West German authorities. This attractively produced book is closely based on the film. It includes a revealing account of their lives which the sisters give in their own words and also contains excellent photographs of Berlin between 1945 and 1989, the majority in black-and-white.

272   **The yellow pimpernels: escape stories of the Berlin Wall.**
Alan Shadrake.   London: Robert Hale, 1974. 160p.

The 'yellow pimpernels' of the title are the people who, for a variety of motives, helped to mastermind the escape across the Berlin Wall of many East Germans after 1961. For further information on the kinds of escape attempts described by Shadrake, see *East European dissent. Volume 1: 1953-1964* and *Volume 2: 1965-1970*, both edited by Vojtech Mastny (New York: Facts on File, 1972).

273   **The ugly frontier.**
David Shears.   New York: Knopf, 1970. 233p.; London: Chatto & Windus, 1970. 231p.

A journalist with the *Daily Telegraph*, Shears sets out to provide what he calls 'the hard physical facts' (p. 7) about the division of Germany rather than another Cold War treatise. He puts the Berlin Wall in perspective as 'just a small section of the border fortifications' which East Germany began constructing as early as 1952. Two chapters (p. 105-18 and p. 193-202) are devoted to the particular effects of the division in Berlin.

274   **Bedrohung und Bewährung.** (Standing firm against the threat.)
Kurt Shell.   Cologne: Opladen, FRG: Westdeutscher Verlag, 1965. 480p.

A perceptive study which has stood the test of time very well. After outlining the way the crisis grew and the attitudes of the various powers involved, Shell deals in depth with the part played by public opinion, not least following the death of Peter Fechter, a young East German cruelly shot and left to die as he tried to cross the Wall.

275   **The Berlin crisis of 1961: Soviet-American relations and the struggle for power in the Kremlin.**
Robert M. Slusser.   Baltimore, Maryland; London: Johns Hopkins University Press, 1973. 510p. bibliog.

Slusser's detailed study focuses on Soviet-American relations between Khrushchev's meeting with Kennedy in Vienna in June 1961 and the Twenty-Second Congress of the Soviet Communist Party in October of the same year. His argument is that, throughout the Berlin crisis of 1961, a power struggle was taking place within the Soviet hierarchy which was far more fierce and potentially dangerous than had hitherto been realised.

276 **The defense of Berlin.**
Jean Edward Smith.   Baltimore, Maryland: Johns Hopkins Press;
London: Oxford University Press, 1963. 431p. maps. bibliog.

Smith provides a comprehensive account of Western efforts to ensure the defence of West Berlin from Communist aggression from the end of the Second World War until the aftermath of the building of the Berlin Wall in 1961. Writing in 1963, he sees the Wall essentially as a victory for the Soviet Union over the Western powers, whose reactions to the events of 13 August 1961 had been too hesitant and cautious. As a result, the status of West Berlin had been fundamentally changed: 'What was formerly an offensive sally port for the Western powers was now, at best, a defensive bastion' (p. 8). His conclusion is that the task of maintaining the freedom of West Berlin has been rendered much more difficult. The volume includes a chronology of events and three maps.

277 **Divided Berlin: the anatomy of Soviet political blackmail.**
Hans Speier.   New York: Praeger; London: Thames & Hudson, 1961.
201p. bibliog.

Speier's short study of the Berlin crisis of 1958-61 is thoughtful and informative but is finally unable to resolve the question of whether it was the Western allies or the Communists who benefited more from the building of the Berlin Wall in August 1961.

278 **The writings on the wall: peace at the Berlin Wall.**
Terry Tillman, foreword by Marilyn Ferguson.   Santa Monica,
California: 22/7 Publishing Company, 1990. 152p.

Excellent colour photographs of the often brilliantly executed paintings on the Berlin Wall, and of the so-called *Mauerspechte* – ordinary people who, after the collapse of the GDR, chipped away at the Wall with hammer and chisel, often in the hope of rescuing a colourful souvenir.

279 **The issues in the Berlin-German crisis.**
Edited by Lyman M. Tondel, Jr.   New York: Oceana Publications,
1963. 80p. bibliog. maps.

The background papers and proceedings of the first Hammarskold Forum organized by the Association of the Bar of the City of New York, 1962.

280 **Wall: the inside story of divided Berlin.**
Peter Wyden.   New York, London, Toronto, Sydney, Tokyo: Simon
& Schuster, 1989. 765p. bibliog.

This blockbuster volume interweaves well-researched political history with the personal, often tragic stories of a small number of Berliners whose lives were deeply affected by the construction of the Wall. The book is based on interviews with over two hundred people, including the writer Stefan Heym, whom the author had first met when they were serving together in the American army during the Second World War. It has a diary-like quality which makes it, in parts at least, a compelling read. It also contains a chronology of main events (1958-87) and numerous photographs.

The Four-Power Agreement (1971-72)

281 **Agreement on Berlin: a study of the 1970 Quadripartite negotiations.**
Dennis L. Bark. Washington, DC: American Enterprise Institute for
Public Policy Research; Stanford, California: Hoover Institution on
War, Revolution and Peace, 1974. 131p. maps. (AEI-Hoover Policy
Study, no. 10).

This analysis of the political process which led to the Quadripartite Agreement on
Berlin in September 1971 attempts to 'adopt to some extent a West Berliner's point of
view'. It sees the solution, or partial solution, of the Berlin problem as depending not
on the Berliners themselves or on the Germans as a whole but on the Four Powers
whose desire for negotiations was tempered by an unwillingness to give ground on their
established positions. While welcoming the Agreement as essential to a much-needed
improvement in East-West relations, Bark criticizes the West for failing to take a
tougher line on the question of the Soviet Consulate-General in West Berlin. The text
of the Agreement and some supporting documents are included in an appendix.

282 **The diplomacy of the Quadripartite Agreement on Berlin: a new era in
East-West politics.**
Honoré M. Catudal Jr., foreword by Kenneth Rush. Berlin (West):
Berlin Verlag, 1977. 335p. bibliog. (Political Studies, no. 12).

A scholarly but readable account of the Four-Power talks which led to the
implementation of the Quadripartite Agreement on Berlin in 1972. Undeterred by the
unavailability of official diplomatic records relating to the agreement, Catudal
constructed the story in outline by using the public sources to which he did have access
and then using his good contacts with key participants to flesh it out and modify it
where appropriate. He sees the agreement both as the main instrument for getting
détente properly underway and also as the best barometer of progress in a new era of
East-West relations. The book also includes an index and photographs.

283 **A balance sheet of the Quadripartite Agreement on Berlin: evaluation
and documentation.**
Honoré Marc Catudal, foreword by Kenneth Rush. Berlin (West):
Berlin Verlag, 1978. 303p. bibliog. (Political Studies, no. 13).

This volume deals with the changes brought about in Berlin by the Quadripartite
Agreement on Berlin reached in 1971. Successive chapters examine the effects on
access controls, railway traffic, waterways traffic, freedom of movement, urban
problems (including telephone communication and mail delivery), and West Berlin's
ties with the Federal Republic of Germany. In a final chapter, Catudal recognises that
tension has been reduced in Berlin but insists that the city continues to act as a
seismograph registering the ups and downs in what he calls 'a shaky détente' (p. 133).
The book includes an index, numerous photographs and figures, and appendices
containing a full English text of the Quadripartite Agreement on Berlin of 3 September
1971, a chronology of events for 1943-78, and a list of tables.

284 **Die Entkrampfung Berlins** *oder* **Eine Stadt geht zur Tagesordnung über.**
(The relaxation of tension in Berlin *or* A city gets down to business.)
Edited by Rolf Heyen. Reinbek, FRG: Rowohlt, 1972. 159p. bibliog.

As its title suggests, this volume welcomes what it sees as the success of the Quadripartite Agreement of 1971 in achieving a higher degree of normality for life in Berlin after a quarter of a century of uncertainty and threats. The book's twenty contributors, including leading politicians (such as Willy Brandt), journalists, and academics, explore a variety of perspectives on Berlin's political and economic future. In an appendix, Hellmut Sieglerschmidt, Jr. chronicles the status of Berlin from 1944 to 1971. Also included are the texts both of the Treaty on Transit Traffic and also of the agreement between West Berlin's Senate and the government of the GDR regarding improved arrangements for West Berliners wishing to visit the GDR.

285 **Berlin im geteilten Deutschland.** (Berlin in divided Germany.)
Dieter Mahncke. Munich, FRG; Vienna: Oldenbourg, 1973. 325p.
bibliog. (Schriften des Forschungsinstituts der deutschen Gesellschaft
für auswärtige Politik e. V., vol. 34).

Written against the background of successful negotiations on the Quadripartite Agreement of 1971, this study displays the widely shared optimism of the day that these discussions would ensure West Berlin a more stable and secure future than had seemed likely in the preceding era. Nevertheless, Mahncke recognizes that the city's situation remained abnormal given its existence as an island within the GDR, the structure of its population, and the psychological pressure on all its citizens. This meant that the continuing vigilance and support of the West were called for in order to ensure that the Soviet Union and the GDR accepted the long-term future of West Berlin. In the early 1970s it was this rather than unification which seemed the most realistic hope for the future. An extensive appendix includes the full text of the Four Power Treaty, the Transit Treaty, agreements between the West Berlin Senate and the government of the GDR, as well as a variety of associated documents (p. 267-306).

286 **Die Einbeziehung Berlins in die europäischen Gemeinschaften unter
besonderer Berücksichtigung des Viermächte-Abkommens über Berlin
vom 3. September 1971.** (The inclusion of Berlin in the European
communities, with particular regard to the Four Power Treaty on Berlin
of 3 September 1971.)
Hartmut Schramm. Frankfurt am Main, FRG; Bern, New York:
Peter Lang, 1986. 173p. map. bibliog.

Writing from the perspective of the mid-1980s, Schramm argues that, in spite of the USSR's protests, Berlin is securely bedded in the European communities. He adds, however, that Western politicians are still faced with the problem of ensuring that Berlin is not forgotten as the pace of European integration continues to quicken. An appendix contains the Four Powers Treaty in its German version as well as other documents in English, French, and German.

287 **Berlin: from symbol of confrontation to keystone of stability.**
James S. Sutterlin, David Klein.   New York; Westport, Connecticut;
London: Praeger, 1989. 232p. bibliog.

Written by two long-serving members of the US Foreign Service who both had major
responsibility for developing US policy during the Four Power negotiations on the
Berlin agreement signed in 1971, this excellent study traces the history of the four
wartime allies' evolving views on the status of Berlin and examines closely how it was
possible to negotiate the agreement without requiring the Western allies on the one
side and the Soviets on the other to sacrifice their longstanding positions of principle.
This clearly involved some fancy diplomatic footwork, as the authors acknowledge in
their preface: 'The Quadripartite Agreement may, indeed, be the only important
international instrument in which the subject is never defined'. In showing how this
was possible, the authors were able, crucially, to use their own recollections, personal
notes, and correspondence. They conclude that the agreement was a victory for all the
negotiating parties and, indeed, for the world, for it provided a more secure peace and
a framework within which the two German states 'are likely to remain discrete but
increasingly integrated' (p. 197). Although the division has in the event been
overcome, this book remains an invaluable study of one of the most important phases
in Berlin's post-War history. The English version of the complete text of the
Quadripartite Agreement, together with associated documents, is provided in an
appendix. There is also an index and a selection of photographs.

288 **The legal status of the Land Berlin: a survey after the Quadripartite
Agreement.**
Ernst R. Zivier, translated from the German by Paul S. Ulrich. Berlin
(West): Berlin Verlag, 1987. 380p. bibliog. index. (Völkerrecht und
Politik 8a).

Contains documents in English translation relating to the complex legal status of
Berlin, including the text of the Quadripartite Agreement (p. 239-359).

The Post-Unification period (1990-)

289 **Hauptstadtsuche: Hauptstadtfunktionen im Interessenkonflikt zwischen
Bonn und Berlin.** (Search for a capital: functions of a capital and the
conflict of interests between Bonn and Berlin.)
Klaus von Beyme.   Frankfurt am Main: Suhrkamp, 1991. 132p.

Von Beyme's book appeared at the height of the debate about whether Bonn or Berlin
should be the seat of government in a newly-united Germany. The author argues that
there is no such thing as a 'natural capital', that capitals are created by political
decisions, and that the current choice between Bonn and Berlin is dramatic
confirmation of this. He outlines the major factors which impinge on that choice,
particularly in the political, economic, and cultural spheres. His thesis is that the
political and cultural spheres are more closely linked and more crucial than the
political and economic, and this conviction underpins his plea at the end of the book
for Berlin as the more appropriate capital *and* seat of government for Germany.

290 **Die Hauptstadtdebatte: der stenographische Bericht des Bundestages.**
(The debate on the capital: the stenographic report of the Bundestag.)
Edited and with a commentary by Helmut Herles. Bonn, Berlin:
Bouvier, 1991. 490p.

Herles makes no secret of his belief that, in choosing between Bonn and Berlin, the
Bundestag reached the wrong decision in making Berlin the capital and the seat of
government of a unified Germany. He thereby provides evidence for the fact that the
decision of 20 June 1991 by no means meant the end of the controversy surrounding
the issue. This volume contains the full text of all the speeches delivered in the debate,
as does a rival, equally accessible publication; *Berlin-Bonn. Die Debatte. Alle Bundes-
tagsreden vom 20. Juni 1991.* (Berlin-Bonn. The debate. All the speeches delivered in
the Bundestag on 20 June 1991) (Edited by the Deutscher Bundestag Referat
Öffentlichkeitsarbeit. Cologne: Kiepenheuer & Witsch, 1991. 653p.).

291 **An obituary for the Berlin Wall.**
James A. McAdams. *World Policy Journal*, vol. 7, no. 2 (1990),
p. 357-75.

Writing in the immediate aftermath of the Berlin Wall's fall, McAdams rightly stresses
the guarded, ambivalent reaction of the allies to this historic event. Whereas the
building of the Wall in 1961, however shocking it originally was, had essentially served
to bring greater clarity into East-West relations and to instil a stronger sense of
coherence into West German foreign policy, its removal opened up a Pandora's box of
uncertainties. McAdams sees a particular threat to the Federal Republic's carefully
nurtured relationships with its neighbours and calls upon the latter to have the trust
and confidence to welcome the new Germany into their fold. He also suggests that,
Berlin Wall or no Berlin Wall, 'East Germany will never completely go away but will
instead, in some undoubtedly uneasy fashion, live on within the body of the new
German state' (p. 368).

292 **Rebirth in Berlin.**
Michael Meyer. *Newsweek* (8 Oct. 1990), p. 38-42.

Meyer lays out the problems but also the opportunities presented by the reunification
of the city after the fall of the Berlin Wall. The main danger appears to be that Berlin
might become 'culturally the most vibrant and exciting city in Europe but economically a
disaster' (Dietrich Stobbe, as quoted by Meyer). Two years after Meyer's article appeared
there seemed no compelling reason to believe that his fears had been banished.

293 **Berlin: der kapitale Irrtum: Argumente für ein föderalistisches
Deutschland.** (Berlin: the capital mistake: arguments for a federalist
Germany.)
Thomas Schmid. Frankfurt am Main, FRG: Eichborn, 1991. 165p.
bibliog.

In his refreshingly combative book Schmid expressly rejects any idea that his approach
to the burning issue of whether Berlin should be the capital of a unified Germany
might be described as balanced. Indeed, his understanding of German history leads
him to reject out of hand all arguments calling for the establishment of Berlin as
Germany's capital. In his estimation, Germany does not need a great capital, for to
have one would be damaging to the country's federal structures, would hinder the
successful unification of the two German states, and would damage Germany's

European ideals. Although Schmid's forcefully-argued views did not in the event carry the day, his book remains an invigorating read.

294 **Berlin: coming in from the cold.**
Ken Smith.   London: Hamish Hamilton, 1990. 240p.;
Harmondsworth: Penguin, 1991. 318p.

An excellent example of well-written 'instant history', Ken Smith's book has all the immediacy and vividness of an eye-witness account of events before and during the unification of Germany and Berlin in 1990. It is also based on journalists' reports, anecdotes, and a canny sense of what the Berliners themselves feel and think. Writing in the immediate aftermath of the Wall's fall, Smith describes West Berlin as a pleasant city under threat from an enormous influx of newcomers and from the high costs which that entails, but his prognosis is essentially a positive one: 'If anyone can work it out, Berliners can' (p. 7). Nevertheless, he concludes that West Berlin's Cold War role as showcase of the West is now clearly at an end and that the city's future remains for the time being a matter of somewhat nervous speculation.

Population

295   **The Berlin population.**
      T. H. Elkins, with B. Hofmeister. In : *Berlin: the spatial structure of a divided city*.   London, New York: Methuen, 1988, p. 215-42.
Writing of divided Berlin little more than a year before the fall of the Wall, Elkins sees the city as an anomaly compared with other European city regions, East or West, in that its population of 5.2 million in 1939 had fallen to at most 3.9 million by 1982. His informative study highlights the population development of Greater Berlin and of West Berlin, paying particular attention to West Berlin's foreign, especially Turkish, population and pointing to the lack of a significant parallel in East Berlin. He also deals with the structure of West Berlin's population and with the demographic and social structure of the districts which made up that half of the divided city. In describing population development in East Berlin, he emphasises that there were virtually no social-spatial contrasts there of the kind found in West Berlin because, in principle, the system of allocating housing was 'highly egalitarian' (p. 239).

296   **The quality of urban life: social, psychological, and physical conditions.**
      Dieter Frick.   Berlin (West): de Gruyter, 1986. 262p. bibliog. index.
One chapter of Frick's fascinating study looks at the Turkish population of West Berlin as a particular example of the problems of integration faced by ethnic minorities in an alien society.

297   **Ich bin wer: Stadtreportagen.** (I am somebody: urban reports.)
      Heinz-Dieter Schilling.   Berlin (West): Express Edition, 1983. 110p.
On the basis of his work as a teacher and adviser of young people, Schilling tells the story of ten foreigners (from Jugoslavia, Chile, Lebanon, Tanzania, France, Israel, Korea, Italy, and two from Turkey) and the difficulties they experience in adapting to life in West Berlin. The book includes ten photographs.

Language

298 **Das neue Berliner Schimpfwörterbuch.** (The new Berlin dictionary of invective.)
Edited by Theodor Constantin.   Berlin (West): Haude & Spener,
1988. 10th ed. 96p. bibliog.

The book provides a rich sample of the disrespectful, sharp-tongued wit (the infamous 'Berliner Schnauze') for which Berliners are justly celebrated. A distinctive feature are the excellent illustrative cartoons by Erich Rauschenbach.

299 **Berliner Wörterbuch.** (Berlin dictionary.)
Peter Schoblinski.   Berlin (West): Edition Marhold, 1986. 281p.
bibliog.

A dictionary of expressions which are a distinctive feature of the Berlin vernacular. Invaluable to anyone who wishes to get below the surface of Berlin life.

300 **Stadtsprache Berlin: eine soziolinguistische Untersuchung.** (The urban language of Berlin: a sociolinguistic study.)
Peter Schoblinski.   Berlin (West), New York: Walter de Gruyter,
1987. 299p. bibliog. (Soziolinguistik und Sprachkontakt/Sociolinguistics and Language Contact, vol. 3).

Based on the author's doctoral dissertation (1985), this is a work for the specialist interested in analysing the particular forms of German which have evolved in Berlin. The book describes itself as a pilot study in an area of research requiring further development.

Society, Health and Welfare

301 **H: autobiography of a child prostitute and heroin addict.**
Edited by Kai Hermann, Horst Rieck, translated from the German by
Susanne Flatauer. London: Arlington Books, 1980. 282p.

Based on tape-recorded interviews made in 1978 by two reporters on *Stern* magazine,
this book tells, in her own words, the chilling story of a teenage girl's addiction to
heroin (or H, as the junkies called it – hence the title of the book). Her account of the
world of drugs and prostitution in Berlin, and of the social and domestic problems
which led to her addiction, caused a sensation in West Germany. This was reinforced
by the film version (entitled *Die Kinder vom Bahnhof Zoo*), which became the biggest
box-office success in the history of the German cinema. With slight amendments, the
book was later made available on the American market under the title *Christiane F:
autobiography of a girl of the streets and heroin addict* (Toronto, New York, London,
Sydney, Auckland: Bantam Books, 1982).

302 **Die Charité: die Geschichte eines Weltzentrums der Medizin.** (The
Charité hospital: the history of a world centre of medicine.)
Gerhard Jaeckel. Bayreuth, FRG: Hestia, 1987. 2nd ed. 584p.

This lively history of Berlin's most famous hospital, which was founded by decree of
Frederick I of Prussia on 14 November 1709 as a response to the Black Death that was
threatening Berlin and Prussia, adopts a popular, non-scholarly approach. It breaks off
in 1945, pausing only to scorn the 'rule of dull functionaries' in the hospital following
the building of the Berlin Wall in 1961 (the hospital stood just inside the eastern,
Communist-ruled part of the city). The book is illustrated with numerous black-and-
white photographs, many of them showing some of the most famous specialists to work
in the Charité, including Rudolf Virchow, August Bier, and Ferdinand Sauerbruch.
The volume has also appeared as an Ullstein paperback (TB 34534).

303 **Ethnic and gender inequality in the labour market: the case of West Berlin and Germany.**
Hermann Kurthen. *Studi Emigrazione*, vol. 28, no. 101, p. 82-111.
Kurthen provides a careful discussion of the ethnic and gender-biased composition of the labour market in Germany and, in particular, in West Berlin. His work is based partly on data from a survey of seventy-nine companies within Berlin's manufacturing industry and partly on the analysis of secondary statistical data. He points out that Germany's original intention when recruiting foreign nationals had been to set up a temporary rotation of migrant labourers, but these had in fact become a permanent segment of West German society. In West Berlin they had come by 1987 to represent 12 per cent of the population and were concentrated in two sectors of industry: manufacturing and services. Women were particularly disadvantaged, while the children of foreign workers were also, for a variety of reasons, unlikely to succeed in German schools or in the workplace. Kurthen describes the situation of foreign workers today as 'an intermediary position', since indications of a gradual integration into the employment system unfortunately go hand in hand with signs of the consolidation of the marginal status of foreigners doing unattractive jobs. Kurthen argues that they should be permitted to have dual citizenship or at least be granted 'landed immigrant status', and he describes any suggestion that they should be excluded or even expatriated as 'difficult to support' (p. 106). He sees a danger of serious conflict arising from the effects of German unification and the possible migration to Germany of millions of people from Eastern Europe and the territory of the former Soviet Union. In this respect he looks to the European Community to settle quickly and fairly the legal and labour market status of Germany's and Berlin's 'guest workers'.

304 **Das Grundwasser in Berlin: Bedeutung, Probleme, Sanierungskonzeptionen.** (Ground-water in Berlin: importance, problems, plans for improvement.)
Rudolf Kloos with the assistance of Wolfgang Frey, Dietrich Jahn, Rüdiger Schober, and Dieter Vogt. Berlin (West): Senator für Stadtentwicklung und Umweltschutz, 1986. 165p. bibliog.
This is the fifth in a series of reports on various themes produced under the auspices of Berlin (West)'s Senator for Civic Development and Environmental Protection and is evidence of the City's concern to protect its sources of drinking water. It follows on from a report on the same subject published in 1977. The volume includes numerous diagrams and a fold-out geological map of West Berlin (1:50,000).

305 **Heroinszene: Selbst- und Fremddefinitionen einer Subkultur.** (Heroine scene: [Self-] Definitions of a sub-culture.)
Peter Nollar, Helmut Reinicke. Frankfurt am Main, FRG; New York: Campus, 1987. 250p. bibliog. (Campus Forschung, vol. 534).
This study of the thought patterns of heroine users, police, doctors and social workers is based on interviews conducted in Berlin and Frankfurt am Main. The authors adopt an approach which they term 'narrative analysis' and see this exemplified in their discussion of an interview with a female junkie in Berlin. The interview is published in full on p. 36-49. A further eight interviews – with junkies, police, social workers, and doctors – are published in an appendix on p. 171-250. On the basis of their analysis the authors conclude that there is an 'an almost irreconcilable confrontation between the

scene and the social institutions' (p. 155-56). In explaining the causes of heroin dependency, the former stress the search for a new identity and the wish to change their social situation, while the latter tend to see the source of confrontation in the junkie's social and subjective deformation.

Politics, Government and the Constitution

306 **The legal status of Berlin.**
I. D. Henry, M. C. Wood. Cambridge, England: Grotius, 1987. 388p. bibliog.

In 1987, the unique legal status of Berlin had remained essentially unchanged since 1945, whatever the alterations to the political context. In the authors' view, the maintenance of that status was essential to the freedom of West Berlin's 1.9 million inhabitants. Their discussion of the problem takes a practical approach, describing the legal position not in abstract terms but as it emerges from the actual positions adopted by the governments and other authorities concerned. Theoretical issues and policy questions are not explored. Within these parameters the book offers a comprehensive and authoritative analysis of its subject. This is divided into seven parts: Berlin and Germany as a whole; Berlin (general); access to Berlin; the ties between Berlin and the Federal Republic; the external representation of Berlin's interests; Berlin (internal); and the Soviet sector of Berlin. In a brief postscript, the authors call for vigilance to preserve Berlin's legal status until the reunification of Germany – a distant goal – (p. 311) can be achieved. As well as an index, the volume also includes a section of documents in English (p. 313-350), maps (p. 351-355), a table of treaties and other principal instruments as well as principal inner-German arrangements (p. 357-361), and a table of legislative measures (p. 362-374).

307 **Die Verfassung von Berlin und das Grundgesetz für die Bundesrepublik Deutschland.** (The constitution of Berlin and the Basic Law for the Federal Republic of Germany.)
Edited by the Landeszentrale für politische Bildungsarbeit Berlin.
Berlin: Landeszentrale für politische Bildungsarbeit, 1991. 91p.

The full text of the constitution of Berlin is published here (p. 3-27) together with a list of the twenty-four changes which have been made to it since it was completed in September 1950 and came into effect a month later. The most recent change was approved on 3 June 1991.

308 **Verfassungsschutz-Bericht: Berlin 1991.** (Report on the protection of the constitution: Berlin 1991.)
Edited by the Landesamt für Verfassungsschutz, foreword by Dieter Heckelmann. Berlin: Landesamt für Verfassungsschutz, 1992. 204p.

Following a similar publication in 1990, this is the second annual report on the activities of the extreme left and the extreme right in Berlin and on the authorities efforts to deal with them. In addition, the report outlines official attempts to uncover the continuing activities of spies once employed by the secret service of the former GDR. Dieter Heckelmann, Berlin's Senator for the Internal Affairs, insists in his foreword that, despite the collapse of Communism in Eastern Europe, important work remains to be done in protecting Berlin's and Germany's democracy. The appendices include brief descriptions of the major extremist organizations and separate chronologies of the main activities of both left-wing and right-wing extremists in Berlin in 1991.

309 **Berlin: development of its government and administration.**
Elmer Plischke with the assistance of Elisabeth Erdmann. Westport, Connecticut: Greenwood, 1970. xii and 257p. bibliog. (Historical Division Monographs).

This book is a reprint of an historical survey originally published in 1952 by the Office of the US High Commissioner for Germany, Historical Division.

Economy

310   **Country to play with: level of industry negotiations in Berlin 1945-46.**
       Alec Cairncross.   Gerards Cross, England: Colin Smythe, 1987. 72p.
In the winter of 1945-46 Alec Cairncross played a leading part in the allied negotiations
in Berlin which discussed the reparations to be exacted from a defeated Germany.
These negotiations led to agreement in March 1946 on a 'Plan for reparations and the
level of Post-War German economy' (sic). Cairncross' short account, which follows
almost verbatim his memoirs which he drafted in 1952, presents a personal view of the
negotiations based on the author's papers and on his personal correspondence at the
time. After leaving Berlin in March 1946, Cairncross submitted a report on the Plan to
the Treasury and the Control Office, but, curiously, little or no attention appears to
have been paid to it and 'I have been unable to trace it in the Public Record Office'
(p. 71). For a more detailed, less personal discussion of the negotiations and the
historical context in which they took place, see Cairncross' book *The price of war:
British policy on German reparations 1941 to 1949* (Oxford: Blackwell, 1986).

311   **The Berlin economy.**
       T. H. Elkins, B. Hofmeister.   In: *Berlin: the spatial structure of a
       divided city*.   London, New York: Methuen, 1988, p. 123-55.
Characterizing the post-War history of West Berlin industry as 'one of disasters from
which, however, recovery was often remarkable' (p. 130), Elkins looks in particular at
its energy supply, its structure, and its tertiary sector. Turning to industry in East
Berlin, he concentrates on its structure, its location, its attempts to ensure proportional
economic development, and its tertiary sector.

312   **The future of the metropolis: Berlin – London – Paris – New York:
       economic aspects.**
       Edited by Hans-Jürgen Ewers, John B. Goddard, Horst Matzerath.
       Berlin (West): De Gruyter, 1986. 484p. bibliog.
The ambitious project which is outlined in this volume was timed to coincide with the
celebrations to mark Berlin's 750th anniversary in 1987 and with the International

Building Exhibition that was part of those celebrations. The purpose of the project was to focus attention on the future of Berlin by comparison with other major world capitals. The four case studies discuss the economic history and problems of the cities in question and discuss the political options which face decision-makers.

313   **Die Hauptstadt Berlin und ihre Wirtschaft.** (East Berlin and its economy.)
      Berthold Fege, Werner Gringmuth, Günter Schulze.   Berlin (East): Verlag Die Wirtschaft, 1987. 240p.

With its emphasis on what it sees as East Berlin's dynamic economic growth, this volume faithfully reflects the ruling SED's optimistic, not to say illusory view of its achievements in the capital and in the country at large. The text is illustrated with numerous black-and-white photographs and figures.

314   **Berliner Steuerpräferenzen: Kommentierung des Berlinförderungsgesetzes.** (Preferential taxes for Berlin: a commentary on the law for the promotion of Berlin.)
      Heinz George.   Wiesbaden, FRG: Forkel, 1983. 6th rev. ed. 618p. bibliog. (Forkel-Reihe Recht und Steuern).

From the early 1950s a variety of special tax privileges was extended to West Berlin by the Federal Republic in recognition both of its economically disadvantageous location as an island within the territory of GDR and also of the political importance of ensuring its level of prosperity did not fall markedly below that of West Germany as a whole. For example, tax concessions to industry were designed to encourage investment in Berlin, Berliners paid lower income tax and corporation tax than West Germans, and employees received on top of their normal salary or wage an additional payment known as the *Berlinzulage*. This volume includes the amended version of the *Berlinförderungsgesetz* (Law on the promotion of Berlin) which was approved on 20 December 1982 and also provides a critical commentary intended to help those, particularly Berliners, who wished to make fruitful application of its provisions. A second volume was published in 1986 under the title *Berliner Steuerpräferenzen. Ergänzungsband 1986 zur 6. Auflage 1983* (Preferential taxes for Berlin. Supplementary volume of 1986 to the 6th edition of 1983) (Wiesbaden, FRG: Forkel), in which account is taken of changes to the law in 1983-86 as well as of other related issues. Following the unification of Germany in October 1990, the Federal Republic quickly set in motion a process by which Berlin will gradually be deprived of its special tax status. See also *Berlinförderungsgesetz mit Verwaltungsanweisungen und Materialen* (Law on the promotion of Berlin, with administrative instructions and additional materials), with a commentary by Hansgeorg Sönksen and Günter Söffing (Berlin [West]: Erich Schmidt, 1973.). This volume is published in a loose-leaf binder, so that it can be constantly brought up to date as the law is amended. For this reason, its pages are numbered by section rather than from beginning to end of the book. In addition to the text of the law itself, the volume contains a lengthy commentary, a section of supporting materials, an index, and a list of abbreviations.

315 **Berlin und seine Wirtschaft: ein Weg aus der Geschichte in die Zukunft: Lehren und Erkenntnisse.** (Berlin and its economy: a path out of history into the future: lessons and insights.)
Edited by the Industrie- und Handelskammer zu Berlin. Berlin (West); New York: de Gruyter, 1987. 256p. bibliog.

This volume assembles a series of twelve lectures which were given by German specialists in 1986-87 at the invitation of the Berlin Chamber of Industry and Commerce. Taken together, they offer a comprehensive overview of Berlin's economic development from the seventeenth century to the middle of the 1980s.

316 **Wirtschaftswunder Berlin?** (Economic miracle Berlin?)
Edited by Klaus Peter Kisker, Michael Heine, introduction by Horst Kramp. Berlin (West): Edition Sigma Bohn, 1987. 265p. bibliog.

The shared purpose of the nine essays contained in this stimulating volume is to challenge what is seen as a widespread, over-optimistic view of West Berlin's economic development in the 1980s.

317 **Work in a nationally owned factory: facts, figures and reports on the NARVA bulb factory in Berlin.**
Klaus Weise, translated from the German by Intertext. Berlin (East): Panorama DDR, 1976. 80p.

This booklet, which includes sixteen pages of plates, has historical value for the insights it affords into the East German view of public ownership, the implementation of economic planning, and the role of the ruling Socialist Unity Party within the factory's operations. The function of the trade unions as a promoter of productivity is described, as is the provision for welfare, education, culture and sport. The situation of working women is also dealt with.

Transport

318   **Transport developments.**
T. H. Elkins, B. Hofmeister.   In: *Berlin: the spatial structure of a
divided city*.   London, New York: Methuen, 1988, p. 99-122.
A succinct analysis of the process by which, despite certain natural disadvantages,
Berlin became from the middle of the nineteenth century onwards a major traffic node
by road, rail, water, and air. Elkins emphasises how, after the Second World War,
West Berlin lost much of its importance in this respect, whereas East Berlin was able
to maintain a more normal relationship with its hinterland and with countries to its
north, east, and south. He devotes individual sections to waterways, railways, road
links, air transport, and urban transportation.

319   **Die S-Bahn in Berlin.** (The overhead railway in Berlin.)
Alfred Gottwaldt (et al.).   Stuttgart, FRG: Kohlhammer/Edition
Eisenbahn, 1988. 128p.
This highly readable study of the overhead railway system which is such a characteristic
feature of Berlin's transport system contains over 150 photographs, including thirty-
three in colour. Also recommended is Peter Bley's *Berliner S-Bahn* (Düsseldorf: Alba,
1991. 5th ed., 168p.) which contains 256 illustrations.

320   **Eisenbahn-Brennpunkt Berlin: die Deutsche Reichsbahn 1920-1939.**
(Railway centre Berlin: the German Reichsbahn 1920-1939.)
Alfred Gottwaldt.   Stuttgart, FRG; Berlin (West), Cologne, Mainz,
FRG: Kohlhammer, 1982. 2nd rev. ed. 155p. bibliog. (Kohlhammer-
Edition Eisenbahn).
A fascinating short history of the railway industry in Berlin, and in particular of the
city's international railway stations, in the two decades from the end of the Second
Empire to the outbreak of the Second World War. The first version of this book
appeared in 1976 (published by Franckh'sche Verlagshandlung in Stuttgart); this
second edition includes ninety extra illustrations (280 in all), replaces fifty photographs

with better ones, and provides a reworked commentary. The same author's book *Berlin. Bahnhof Zoo. Fernbahnhof für eine halbe Stadt* (Düsselforf, FRG: Alba, 1988. 143p. bibliog.) tells the story from 1882 to 1988 of what is today Berlin's best-known railway station, Bahnhof Zoo, which, together with KaDeWe (the exclusive department store Kaufhaus des Westens at Wittenbergplatz), Kempinskis (a hotel on the Kurfürstendamm, Berlin's main shopping street), Café Kranzler, and the Europa-Center, became a major landmark for those visiting the western half of the city whilst Berlin remained divided (1961-89). Less fortunate has been the Anhalter station (dating back to 1839-40), which survived the war only as a ruin but which many would like to see restored to its former glory (*see also* Peter G. Kliem and Klaus Noack, *Berlin. Anhalter Bahnhof*, Frankfurt am Main, FRG; Berlin (West); Vienna: Ullstein, 1984. 112p.).

321 **Berliner Omnibusse.** (Berlin omnibuses.)
Dieter Grammrath, Heinz Jung.   Düsseldorf, FRG: Alba, 1988. 144p.

This history of the omnibus in Berlin takes full account of the different developments which took place in East and West Berlin during the period of the city's post-War division. It also contains numerous photographs, some in colour.

322 **Personenschiffahrt auf Spree und Havel.** (Passenger-boat trips on the Spree and the Havel.)
Kurt Groggert.   Berlin (West): Nicolai, 1988. 345p. bibliog. (Berliner Beiträge zur Technikgeschichte und Industriekultur, vol. 10).

Groggert provides detailed information on the passenger-carrying ships which have plied Berlin and its district's many waterways over two centuries and especially since the close of the nineteenth century, when excursions by steamer became a favourite form of relaxation for Berlin's working population. The volume includes an index listing every ship named in the text and contains approximately 250 photographs, of which thirty-two are in colour.

323 **Verkehr in Berlin: von den Anfängen bis zur Gegenwart.**
(Transport in Berlin: from the beginnings to the present.)
Edited by Landesbildstelle Berlin, introduction by Wilhelm van Kampen.   Berlin (West): Haude & Spener, 1988. 2nd. rev. ed.
vol. 1: Nahverkehr. vol. 2: Fernverkehr.

For these two volumes Jürgen Grothe selected a total of 327 black-and-white photographs from the extensive collection at the *Landesbildstelle*, Berlin's central archive for photographic, audio and film documents. The book lays no claim to provide a systematic historical account of transport in Berlin but it does succeed in giving a vivid visual impression of the changing face of public transport in Berlin from its modest beginning in 1688 when the carriers of twenty-four sedan chairs were given a licence to ply their trade (vol. 1) to the development of links by road, air and water by which Berlin asserted its importance as a trading centre (vol. 2) The address of the Landesbildstelle is D-1000 Berlin 21, Wikingerufer 7.

324 **Berliner U-Bahn.** (Berlin underground railway.)
Ulrich Lemke, Uwe Poppel. Düsseldorf, FRG: Alba, 1985. 7th rev. ed.
160p.

On 15th February 1902 the first-ever journey on Berlin's U-Bahn took place,
transporting numerous representatives from public life, including the Prussian Minister
of Public Works, from Stralauer Tor to Potsdamer Platz, a distance of six kilometres.
Three days later the system was opened to the public. This generously-illustrated
volume tells the story of the railway's development since that first journey and includes
a table showing the names of all the stations and other relevant details. A further
revised edition of this useful book is called for to take account of the expansion of the
railway system following German unification in 1990.

Education and Training

325 **An institute for an empire: the Physikalisch-Technische Reichsanstalt 1871-1918.**
David Cahan. Cambridge, England; New York; New Rochelle, New York; Melbourne, Australia; Sydney: Cambridge University Press, 1989. 315p. bibliog.

The Physikalisch-Technische Reichsanstalt (Imperial Institute of Physics and Technology) came to represent, in another sphere, the German Reich's newly acquired political power and authority. It soon found imitators elsewhere in Germany and abroad, for example in Britain, which set up the National Physical Laboratory in Teddington. Originally written as a dissertation, this is the first scholarly study devoted to the Imperial Institute. It pursues in particular two interrelated themes: the institutionalization of science and technology as exemplified by the Institute; and measurement as the 'essence' of the Institute. In doing so, it combines both a chronological and an analytical approach. The book contains photographs, diagrams, figures, and a list of abbreviations.

326 **Juristenausbildung in Berlin: die Ausbildungsvorschriften in der Neufassung 1985 mit Erläuterungen.** (The training of lawyers in Berlin: the training regulations in the new version of 1985, with commentary.) Manfred Herzig, Klaus Schach. Berlin (West), New York: de Gruyter, 1985. 2nd rev. ed. 235p.

Given the acknowledged importance of the legal profession in German society, it is not surprising that the issue of legal training has always been controversial. As Herzig and Schach note, no set of regulations has managed to survive unchanged for ten years in post-War West Berlin, and each reform makes the rules according to which students of law are trained and examined ever more detailed and complicated. The present volume sets out and provides a commentary on the reformed rules governing the teaching and examining of students of law in West Berlin with effect from the summer semester of 1985.

327 **Friedrich Schleiermacher and the founding of the University of Berlin: the study of religion as a scientific discipline.**
Edited by Herbert Richardson.   Lewiston, New York; Queenston, Ontario; Lampeter, Wales: Edward Mellen Press, 1991. 141p. bibliog. (Schleiermacher Studies and Translations, vol. 5).

In his preface to this volume Herbert Richardson states that Friedrich Schleiermacher's scientific method for analysing religion created the basis for the modern scientific university, as represented by the university established in Berlin in 1809-10. This proposition is then explored in four essays, by Edwina Lawler, Terrence N. Tice, Joseph W. Pickle, and Albert L. Blackwell.

328 **The Free University of Berlin: a political history.**
James F. Tent.   Bloomington, Indianapolis: Indiana University Press, 1988. 507p. bibliog.

Tent analyses the political evolution of the Free University from its origins in 1944 and its founding in 1948 to the late 1980s. His study does not, therefore, deal with the university's scholarly and scientific achievements. He pays particular attention to two phases in the university's development; its founding in 1948 as the Cold War emerged, and the period of the 1960s when it became a focal point for the student movement.

329 **Ingenieure aus Berlin: 300 Jahre technisches Schulwesen.** (Engineers from Berlin: 300 years of technical schools.)
Hans Joachim Wefeld.   Berlin (West): Haude & Spener, 1988. 616p. bibliog.

Wefeld's study offers a detailed, illustrated history of technical education in Berlin from 1640 until the mid-1980s.

330 **Germany's past contested: the Soviet-American conflict in Berlin over history curriculum reform, 1945-48.**
Gregory P. Wegner.   *History of Education Quarterly*, vol. 30, no. 1 (spring 1990), p. 1-16.

In June 1948 the Allied Kommandatura Education Committee signed a little-known four-power pact on the reform of the history curriculum in Berlin's schools. This made the city 'the only area within the entire occupation zone where Soviet and American education officers established a dialogue over a specific dimension of school knowledge' (p. 1). Unfortunately, this remarkable agreement, which was reached against all the odds at a time when relations between the occupation powers were otherwise characterized by constant tensions, occurred only one week before the start of the Berlin Blockade and therefore could never come into effect.

331 **The enlightened soldier: Scharnhorst and the Militärische Gesellschaft in Berlin, 1801-1805.**
Charles Edward White.   New York; Westport, Connecticut; London: Praeger, 1989. 244p. bibliog.

This is a scholarly study of Scharnhorst's leading role in the reform of the Prussian army following its disastrous defeats at the hands of the French at Jena and Auerstedt in 1806. As head of the *Militärische Gesellschaft* (Military Society) from 1801, Scharnhorst was able to push through the idea that soldiering was no longer a craft but a profession requiring serious study, and this certainly helps to explain why the Prussian army was successful during the Wars of Liberation (1813-15), a recovery which, in view of the catastrophic defeats of 1806, White descibes as one of the most remarkable feats in military history.

Statistics

332 **Jewish conversions – a measure of assimilation? A discussion of the Berlin secession statistics of 1770-1941.**
Peter Honigmann, translated from the German, edited and with appendix by Lux Furtmüller. *Leo Baeck Institute Year Book*, vol. 34 (1989), p. 3-45.

Noting that Jewish conversions are usually explained as an aspect of the process of assimilation, Honigmann argues that political pressures on Jews at identifiable points in history constitute a second major determinant, the importance of which has generally been underestimated. He takes a fresh, critical look at the statistical evidence relating to Berlin and draws insightful comparisons with the situation in Vienna and Budapest before coming to the conclusion that, at times of historical crisis (1919, 1933, 1938), political events clearly played a decisive role in increasing the conversion rate and that, even during less turbulent times, comparatively undramatic political pressures exercised a major influence throughout the 171 years covered by his survey. In a useful appendix Lux Furtmüller develops an elementary mathematical procedure in order to investigate the value of the 1939 German census as a source for the comparison of the degrees of assimilation of the Jewish population in Berlin and Vienna.

333 **Die kleine Berlin-Statistik 1991.** (A booklet of statistics on Berlin 1991.) Edited by Landeszentrale für politische Bildungsarbeit Berlin. Berlin: Statistisches Landesamt Berlin, 1991. [64p.]

This booklet, which appears annually, provides basic statistical information on the structure and development of Berlin's economy and society. This issue represents the first attempt after the unification of Berlin to present a picture of the whole city.

334 **Berliner Bezirke: statistisches Taschenbuch.** (The districts of Berlin: statistical pocket-book.)
Edited by Statistisches Landesamt Berlin, foreword by Günther Appel. Berlin: Kulturbuch-Verlag [1991]. 157p.

This useful, pocket-sized booklet represents the first attempt after German unification to compile a statistical survey of a unified Berlin. Given the methodological difficulty or impossibility of reconciling existing statistics from the old East and West Berlin in certain areas, the survey limits itself to those topics where such problems are least in evidence. The data relate in the main to 1989. Following the establishment in autumn 1990 of new, national guidelines for the collation of statistical data, future editions of this publication will be more comprehensive in scope and, in an important sense, more reliable in that the data for all parts of Berlin will derive from a single set of procedures. In addition to a clear presentation of the statistical material, the booklet offers a brief introduction to each of Berlin's twenty-three administrative districts (p. 10-32).

335 **Statistisches Jahrbuch 1991.** (Statistical yearbook 1991.)
Edited by Statistisches Landesamt Berlin. Berlin: Kulturbuch Verlag, 1991. 556p.

This is the official statistical survey of Berlin for 1991. A similar survey appears annually and is an indispensable guide for anyone with a serious interest in the German capital.

Literature

336   The poets of the Café des Westens: Blass, Heym, Hoddis, Lichtenstein.
Edited by Patrick Bridgwater.   Leicester, England: Leicester
University Press, 1984. 96p. bibliog. (Leicester German Poets).

Patrick Bridgwater provides an excellent introduction and notes to his selection from
the works of perhaps the four most important of the poets of early German
Expressionism. For a detailed study of Expressionism in Berlin, see Roy F. Allen,
Literary life in German Expressionism and the Berlin circles (Ann Arbor, Michigan:
UMI Research Press, 1983. 2nd rev. ed. 404p. bibliog.) (Studies in the Fine Arts. The
Avant-Garde, 25).

337   Poet of Expressionist Berlin: the life and work of Georg Heym.
Patrick Bridgwater.   London: Libris, 1991. 305p. bibliog.

This biographical and critical study of the work of the poet Georg Heym (1887-1912) is
aimed at both students and the general reader. Quotations from Heym's work are
given in English, but the poems are also produced in the original German. Georg
Heym, who must be regarded as one of the major figures in German Expressionism,
drowned at the tragically early age of twenty-five when ice-skating on the Havel.

338   The spy who came in from the cold.
John le Carré.   London: Hodder & Stoughton, 1990. 219p. (Coronet
Books).

Originally published in 1963 (London: Victor Gollancz), le Carré's classic spy story
begins and ends with a brutal shooting at the Berlin Wall. Set against the background
of the Cold War which was at its height in the early 1960s, the novel became an
international best-seller and has been translated into more than fifty languages. It is
estimated that, by the end of 1990, over one hundred million copies had been sold
worldwide. Richard Burton starred in the successful film version which was made in
1965 and directed by Martin Ritt. Further important examples of the spy story with a
Berlin background are Len Deighton's novels *Funeral in Berlin* (turned into a film
starring Michael Caine as the central character, Harry Palmer) and *Berlin game*

Literature

(London: Hutchinson, 1983), which also opens and closes with a scene at the Wall Ted Allbeury is another espionage writer to have used divided Berlin as a backdrop notably in *The seeds of treason* (London: Hodder & Stoughton, 1988. 312p.) (New English Library Paperback), in which MI6's Head of Station in West Berlin falls in love with the wife of his opposite number in the KGB in East Berlin and then struggles to extricate them both from the web of international intrigue in which they are enmeshed.

339 **Winter: a novel of a Berlin family.**
Len Deighton. New York: Knopf, 1987. 571p. Also published as
Winter: a Berlin family 1899-1945, London: Hutchinson, 1987. 536p.

The story of a Berlin family and, in particular, of two brothers, Peter and Paul Winter whose lives are shaped by the major developments in German history during the first forty-five years of the twentieth century, not least the rise and fall of the Nazis. An excellent example of popular fiction set against the background of events in Germany and especially Berlin. A paperback edition, published by Grafton Books (London Glasgow, Toronto, Sydney, Auckland: Collins, 1988), somewhat curiously described the novel as 'the fourth book in the trilogy' (!), a reference to Deighton's *Game, set and match* trilogy of spy stories set in the 1980s.

340 **Berlin Alexanderplatz: the story of Franz Biberkopf.**
Alfred Döblin, translated from the German by Eugene Jolas.
Harmondsworth, England: Penguin, 1978. 478p. (Penguin Modern
Classics).

Döblin's classic novel, centred round its proletarian protagonist Franz Biberkopf reveals the intimate knowledge of Berlin's low life which the author had gained whilst a doctor in one of the poorer parts of the city. The novel first appeared in 1929 published by Fischer in Berlin, and this translation was originally entitled *Alexanderplatz* (New York: Viking Press; London: Secker, 1931). For perceptive comment on this and other of Döblin's Berlin novels, see David B. Dollenmayer, *The Berlin novels of Alfred Döblin: 'Wadzek's battle with the steam turbine', 'Berlin Alexanderplatz', 'Men without mercy' and 'November 1918'* (Berkeley, California; London: University of California Press, 1988. 216p. bibliog.); Henrietta S. Schoonover, *The humorous and grotesque elements in Döblin's Berlin Alexanderplatz* (Berne, Switzerland; Las Vegas, Nevada: Lang, [1977]. 280p. bibliog. European University Papers: series 1, German Language and Literature, vol. 178.); and A. F. Bance, 'Alfred Döblin's *Berlin Alexanderplatz* and literary modernism', in *Weimar Germany. Writers and politics*, edited by A. F. Bance (Edinburgh: Scottish Academic Press, 1982, p. 53-64). The script of and other information on the remarkable film of the book which was made by Rainer Werner Fassbinder can be found in Rainer Werner Fassbinder, Harry Baer *Der Film Berlin Alexanderplatz. Ein Arbeitsjournal* (The film Berlin Alexanderplatz. A work journal.) (Frankfurt am Main, FRG: Zweitausendeins, 1980. 575p.).

341 **Before the storm: a novel of the winter of 1812-13.**
Theodor Fontane, translated from the German and edited with an
introduction by R. J. Hollingdale. Oxford, New York: Oxford
University Press, 1985. 712p. bibliog.

This is a brilliantly-translated historical novel by one of Germany's greatest writers and one particularly associated with Prussia and its capital, Berlin. Other works by Fontane in English translation are *Effi Briest*, translated by Douglas Parmée, Harmondsworth,

England: Penguin, 1967, reprinted 1976; *A suitable match* (Irrungen Wirrungen), translated by Sandra Morris (London, Glasgow: Blackie, 1968); *Stine*, translated by Harry Steinhauer, in *Twelve German novellas*, edited by Harry Steinhauer (Los Angeles: University of California Press, 1977, p. 315-96); *The woman taken in adultery* and *The Poggenpuhl family*, translated and with notes by Gabriele Annan, introduction by Erich Heller (Chicago, London: University of Chicago Press, 1979. 231p.). The former is also available as *L'Adultera*, translated and with an introduction by Lynn R. Eliason (New York, Bern, Frankfurt am Main, Paris: Peter Lang, 1990. 205p. [American University Studies, Series 1; Germanic Languages and Literature Vol. 90]); *Short novels and other short writings*, edited by Peter Demetz, foreword by Peter Gay (New York: Continuum, 1982, 336p.) (contains *A man of honor*, translated by E. M. Valk: originally published under this title by Frederick Unger, New York, 1975, 206p. bibliog.; *Jenny Treibel*, translated by Ulf Zimmermann: originally published under this title by Frederick Unger, New York, 1976. 209p. notes and introduction by Ulf Zimmermann. bibliog.; and *The eighteenth of March* translated by Krishna Winston).

342 **The changing consciousness of reality: the image of Berlin in selected German novels from Raabe to Döblin.**
Marilyn Sibley Fries.   Bonn: Bouvier, 1980. 183p. bibliog. (Studien zur Germanistik, Anglistik und Komparatistik, vol. 77).

This is a perceptive study of the fictional presentation of Berlin by six German authors of the nineteenth and twentieth centuries: Wilhelm Raabe; Theodor Fontane; Clara Viebig; Georg Hermann; Hans Fallada; and Alfred Döblin. It is Döblin's *Berlin Alexanderplatz* which Fries judges to be the most successful of the nine texts she analyses in 'the creation of the city image' (p. 173).

343 **Berlin: literary images of a city: eine Großstadt im Spiegel der Literatur.**
Edited by Derek Glass, Dietmar Rösler, John J. White.   Berlin (West): Erich Schmidt Verlag, 1989. 219p. bibliog. (Publications of the Institute of Germanic Studies, University of London, vol. 42).

The ten papers in this volume, of which half are in German, were originally delivered at an international conference held in London in 1987. In exploring some aspects of Berlin as a literary *topos*, the authors – all specialists on German literature – concentrate on the nineteenth and twentieth centuries. In the process they bring out some of the conflicting views and versions of the city, revealing it, in the words of the editors in their introduction, to be 'a more heterogeneous entity, more of a conundrum even than Paris, London or New York'. The volume concludes with an excellent select bibliography (p. 188-210).

344 **Literarisches Leben in Berlin: Aufklärer und Romantiker.**
(Literary life in Berlin: Enlightenment and Romanticism.)
Klaus Hermsdorf.   Berlin (East): Akademie, 1987. 456p. bibliog.

Klaus Hermsdorf's perceptive and wide-ranging study focuses on Berlin's importance as a European centre of literary life since the middle of the eighteenth century.

345 **Mr. Norris changes trains. Goodbye to Berlin.**
Christopher Isherwood, introduction by James Fenton.   London:
Chatto & Windus, 1985. 390p.

The two works included in this volume were originally published in 1935 and 1939 respectively. The first has been described as the first spy novel to be set in Berlin. The second formed the basis of two films, *I am a camera* (a quotation from the opening of the book) and the later, highly popular remake with Liza Minelli, *Cabaret*. Isherwood's fascination with the feverish political and moral atmosphere in the Berlin of the later 1920s and early 1930s did much to establish the image of Berlin in later years.

346 **Fabian: the story of a moralist.**
Erich Kästner, translated from the German by Cyrus Brooks,
introduction by Rodney Livingstone.   London: Libris, 1990. xxiv and
178p. bibliog.

Kästner's satirical novel, which he defined as 'a highly moral book' whose purpose was to warn Germany of the abyss into which it was in danger of falling, succeeds in evoking the frenetic atmosphere of Berlin in the last years of the Weimar Republic between the Wall Street crash and Hitler's accession to power. First published in 1931 in Germany (Stuttgart: Deutsche Verlagsanstalt) and in 1932 in Britain (London: Jonathan Cape), the novel presents a frank picture of morals in contemporary Berlin which the political right found offensive. Indeed, it was one of the books which fell victim to the Nazi's book-burning on Berlin's Opernplatz on 10 May 1933. The sexually explicit passages which Cyrus Brooks had omitted from his otherwise excellent translation in 1932 are restored in the Libris edition. The only other changes to the translation are of a minor nature. The volume also includes the epilogue which had been rejected by the original publisher as well as the new preface which Kästner wrote for the 1950 German reprint.

347 **Emil and the detectives.**
Erich Kästner, translated from the German by Eileen Hall, illustrated
by Walter Trier, introduction by Walter de la Mare.   London:
Jonathan Cape, 1959. 190p.

Kästner achieved fame in 1928 with the publication of *Emil and the detectives*, the first of his many books for children. The Berlin studios of UFA turned it into a film two years later, the script being written by Kästner, Emil Pressburger, and Billy Wilder. The English translation of the book appeared in New York in the same year and in London in 1931. The 1959 re-issue is a new translation by Eileen Hall. Kästner's charming text tells the story of Emil Tischbein, a young boy from the provinces who travels to Berlin to spend a week with relatives and has his money stolen on the train by the man with whom he shares his compartment, Grundeis. Fortunately, he is able to pursue Grundeis through the streets of Berlin with the help of a gang of Berlin children (the 'detectives' of the title). The thief is finally arrested, Emil's exploits are written up in the newspaper, and he earns a substantial reward with which he is able to buy a coat and a hair-dryer for his widowed mother.

348 **Death in Berlin.**
     M. M. Kaye.   Harmondsworth, England: Penguin, 1986. 255p.

This readable thriller, written by the wife of a British army officer temporarily stationed in Berlin, is set in the city in 1953. It was first published by the Staples Press in 1955 under the title *Death walked in Berlin*.

349 **When Hitler stole pink rabbit.**
     Judith Kerr.   London: HarperCollins, 1991. 17th ed. 192p.

First published in 1971, this basically autobiographical story presents an affectionate and often humorous portrait of a Jewish family forced to flee from Hitler's Germany. Judith Kerr's father was Alfred Kerr, one of Berlin's foremost theatre critics before and during the Weimar Republic. The book tells how Kerr first escaped to Prague, then joined his family in Switzerland, before moving on to Paris in the hope of making a living there. As the book closes in 1935, the family has just moved on to England, Kerr having managed to sell a film script there. A second volume, *The other way round* (London: Collins, 1975), focuses on how the family survived the war in London, while a third, *A small person far away* (London: Collins, 1978; revised edition 1989), deals with the post-War period. The appearance of Alfred Kerr's collected works in German inspired his children, Judith and Michael, to found an Alfred Kerr Prize of DM10,000 to be awarded annually to an outstanding young actor or actress. The 1991 award to the first winner, Steffi Kühnert, represented for Judith Kerr 'a kind of return home to Berlin' for her father, who had died in 1948 on his first official visit to Germany after his exile.

350 **Best-sellers by design: Vicki Baum and the house of Ullstein.**
     Lynda J. King.   Detroit, Michigan: Wayne State University Press, 1988. 252p. bibliog.

Vicki Baum wrote a series of bestselling novels for the Berlin-based publishing house of Ullstein. Her big international hit was *Menschen im Hotel* (*Grand Hotel* in the English version. See also the Hollywood film of the same name starring Greta Garbo, John and Lionel Barrymore). A musical based on the novel was written by Luther Davis, Robert Wright and George Forrest and performed in Berlin's Theater des Westens in its 1990/91 season (starring Leslie Caron) – further evidence of the enduring fascination of Baum's work and of its significance as a major cultural document of the Weimar era.

351 **The innocent *or* The special relationship.**
     Ian McEwan.   London: Jonathan Cape; London: Pan Books, 1990. 245p. (Picador Paperback).

Set against the background of Berlin in the 1950s when the Cold War was at its height, this brilliant novel revolves around an ordinary London post-office worker, Leonard Marnham, who becomes involved first in the Anglo-American attempt to build a secret tunnel from the district of Rudow into the Russian sector and then in the gruesome murder and dismemberment of his German fiancée's former husband. He is never brought to book for this crime because, in a superbly ironic twist to the plot, he succeeds in duping the master-spy George Blake without really meaning to (Blake and William Harvey are the only characters taken from real life in this fictional *tour de force*). McEwan has said that he found a brief reference to the tunnel in Peter Wright's *Spycatcher*, but he acknowledges in the book his particular debt to David C. Martin's study of the construction of the tunnel in his book *Wilderness of Mirrors* (New York:

Literature

Harper and Row, 1980. 236p.) McEwan's novel was also published by Doubleday (New York, Toronto, London, Sydney, Auckland, 1990) and by Bantam (New York, Toronto, London, Sydney, Auckland, 1991).

352 The eye.
Vladimir Nabokov.   London: Penguin, 1992. 103p.

Written in Berlin in 1930, where Nabokov lived from 1922 to 1940 as an émigré from Bolshevik Russia, and first published in Russian in 1965, this English version originally appeared, also in 1965 in three instalments in *Playboy*. The story takes place in Berlin in 1924-25 and the protagonists are what Nabokov calls in his foreword 'the favourite characters of my literary youth: Russian expatriates living in Berlin, Paris or London'. As the author somewhat playfully admits, however, they might just as well have been anyone living anywere, for he is (he says) essentially indifferent to the social problems of a particular place and to the intrusions of history. Nevertheless, it is noteworthy that Nabokov wrote seven major works while living in Berlin in the 1920s and that all are set in the city.

353 Our street: a chronicle written in the heart of Fascist Germany.
Jan Petersen, translated from the German and with a foreword by Betty Rensen.   London: Victor Gollancz, 1938. 287p.

The street referred to in the title of this novel is Wallstraße in a working-class area of Berlin-Charlottenburg, but Petersen claims that the events he describes are typical of what happens in similar streets all over Germany. His book, he says, describes the courage of tens of thousands of nameless proletarian heroes who struggled to defeat Fascism and to bring about Socialism. It is prefaced by a list of the eighteen Charlottenburg anti-fascists who lost their lives in the conflict. Indeed, Petersen's original intention was to record the events that took place in Charlottenburg between January 1933 and June 1934, but his chronicle turned into a novel when he realised he would have to protect his comrades and himself from detection by the Nazis. As the translator explains in her foreword, the manuscript of the book had to be smuggled out of Germany at considerable risk to Petersen's life. The volume contains a section of notes which explains German references to an English-speaking readership (p. 281-87).

354 Berlin.
Theodor Plievier, translated from the German by Louis Hagen.
London: Panther, 1969. 478p.; St. Albans, England: Mayflower Books, 1976. 478p.

Plievier's strongly anti-Communist novel opens in April 1945 as the Second World War moves towards its bloody conclusion in the battle for Berlin. It ends with the Workers' Uprising of 17 June 1953 in the eastern half of the divided city. Plievier makes clear his utter contempt for the Ulbricht group which returned to Berlin from Moscow in 1945 to run the Russian occupation zone and its successor, East Germany. Walter Ulbricht himself is the particular object of his venom: 'He left without a beard; he returns sprouting a goatee, and that appears to be the sum total he has achieved during emigration' (p. 261). A recent German edition is Theodor Plievier, *Berlin*, edited by Hans-Harald Müller (Cologne: Kiepenheuer & Witsch; 1985. 610p.). This includes an informative afterword by the editor.

355 **Berlin, ach Berlin.** (Berlin, oh Berlin.)
Edited by Hans Werner Richter.   Munich, FRG: DTV, 1984. 220p.
This volume assembles texts by twenty-four contemporary authors on the theme of
Berlin.

356 **German encounters with modernity: novels of Imperial Berlin.**
Katherine Roper.   New Jersey, London: Humanities Press
International, 1991. 269p. bibliog.
Katherine Roper's scholarly, insightful study sees the novels of Imperial Berlin as an
important historical source which demonstrates Germany's attempts to come to terms
with the new experiences of nationhood and modernity. On the basis of her reading of
130 novels, she selects about fifty for analysis, among them works by Theodor
Fontane, Friedrich Spielhagen, and Max Kretzer.

357 **The wall jumper.**
Peter Schneider, translated from the German by Leigh Hafrey.   New
York: Pantheon Books, 1983; London: Allison & Busby, 1984. 139p.
This widely acclaimed, largely autobiographical novel explores the contrasting
mentalities which developed in East and West Berlin as a consequence of the Cold
War. The narrator, a West German who moved to Berlin shortly after the erection of
the Wall, comes to a conclusion which proved to be well-founded after the Wall finally
came down in 1989: 'It will take us longer to tear down the Wall in our heads than any
wrecking company will need for the Wall we can see' (p. 119). As a writer, he is
interested in finding the story of someone who knows both halves of the city well,
rejects the very different identities which each half offers him, and therefore 'feels at
home only on the border' (p. 23). The novel ends without his having discovered such a
person, however, and all the evidence which the novel presents suggests that the
thinking of Berliners East and West has been conditioned by the state in which they
happen to live. The novel alludes to the experiences of various 'wall jumpers' (people
who found ways of getting across the wall) as well as to the celebrated Biermann affair
of 1976 and the exclusion of nine dissident writers from the East Berlin Writers Union
in 1979, both of which led to the exodus to the West of many of the GDR's leading
writers.

358 **Exit Berlin.**
Tim Sebastian.   London, New York, Toronto, Sydney, Auckland:
Bantam, 1992. 223p.
This is perhaps the first espionage novel to have been published which focuses on
Berlin after the fall of the Wall. It explores with some skill the dangers to which a
British agent is exposed under the radically changed circumstances of post-1989
Germany.

359 **Armageddon.**
Leon Uris.   Garden City, New York: Doubleday, 1964. 632p.;
London: Transworld, 1992. 603p. (Corgi Books).
Originally published in 1964, this bestseller is set against the background of the origins
of the Cold War in post-War Berlin and focuses particularly on the successful Berlin
Airlift of 1948-49, which is seen as a decisive moment in the struggle between East and

Literature

West. The novel is also interesting for its impressive depiction of the chaos and hunger which characterized Berlin at the time of the lift. Its comments on the character of the Germans are perhaps more controversial today than when it was first published.

360 **The captain of Köpenick.**
Carl Zuckmayer, translated from the German by David Portman.
London: Geoffrey Bles, 1932. 171p.

Zuckmayer's celebrated play is based on the true story of an ex-convict, Wilhelm Voigt, who discovered that, by wearing a uniform picked up from a second-hand clothes shop, he was transformed from a victim of Prussian officials into someone with undisputed authority over them. The play was in the programme of the Berliner Ensemble for the 1990/91 season, proof of its enduring appeal. This edition includes two photographs of Voigt and two of the actor Werner Krauss, who played the part of Voigt in a famous production by the Deutsches Theater in Berlin. Köpenick is one of the twenty-three districts which make up today's Berlin.

The Arts

361 **Berlin porcelain.**
Winfried Baer, translated from the German by Erika D. Passantino.
Washington, DC: Smithsonian Institution Press, 1980. 95p.
This is the catalogue of an exhibition of Berlin porcelain, organized by the Staatliche
Porzellan Manufaktur Berlin and the Smithsonian Institution Traveling Exhibition
Service.

362 **Raoul Hausmann and Berlin Dada.**
Timothy O. Benson.   Ann Arbor, Michigan: UMI Research Press,
1987. 280p. bibliog. (Studies in the Fine Arts. The Avant-Garde, 55).
This is a good account of the flowering of Dadaism in Berlin and of Hausmann's
important role in it. The volume can be usefully read in conjunction with the collection
of manifestos and other Dada texts in *Dada Berlin: Texte, Manifeste, Aktionen* (Edited
by Karl Riha. Stuttgart: Reclam, 1977. 184p. bibliog. [RUB 9857]).

363 **Das Orchester: die Innenwelt der Berliner Philharmoniker.**
(The orchestra: the Berlin Philharmonic seen from within.)
Dieter Blum, Emanuel Eckardt.   Stuttgart: Scripta, 1983. 228p.
bibliog.
Between March 1981 and January 1983 the photographer Dieter Blum accompanied
the Berlin Philharmonic Orchestra on its concert tours across the world. In October
1981 he was joined by the journalist Emanuel Eckardt, their joint aim being to
produce a record of the orchestra's work which would afford the reader a demystifying
glimpse behind the scenes (tensions and conflicts are not concealed) while at the same
time celebrating the orchestra's musical achievements.

364   **Cut-steel and Berlin iron jewellery.**
      Anne Clifford.   Bath, England: Adams & Dart, 1971. 95p. bibliog.
Berlin iron jewellery was first manufactured in 1804 in the Royal Berlin Factory, located behind the grounds of the Charité hospital. It was intended both to be attractive and also to emphasis that 'the wearer had been patriotic and sacrificed her gold for the Fatherland' at the time of the wars against Napoleon (p. 12). As Anne Clifford points out in her informative book, this unusual jewellery remained popular until the middle of the nineteenth century and was made in France as well as in Germany. The book contains fifty-seven black-and-white photographs and four in colour.

365   **Theatre for the people: the story of the Volksbühne.**
      Cecil W. Davies.   Manchester, England: Manchester University Press, 1977. 181p. bibliog.
Davies's book provides an authoritative account of the history and achievements of the *Volksbühne*, a unique attempt to bring theatre to a mass audience. Founded in Berlin in 1890 as a subscription organization, the *Volksbühne* idea has since spread to many towns across Germany.

366   **Berlin: culture and metropolis.**
      Charles W. Haxthausen, Heidrun Suhr.   Minneapolis, Minnesota; Oxford: University of Minnesota Press, 1990. 226p. bibliog.
Essentially the product of an international, interdisciplinary conference held in Minneapolis in October 1987 to mark Berlin's 750th anniversary in that year, this stimulating volume combines twelve essays whose shared focus is on 'the often uneasy relationship between twentieth-century Berlin and the culture produced there – in literature, poetry, film, cabaret, and the visual arts'.

367   **Welcome to Berlin: das Image Berlins in der englischsprachigen Welt von 1700 bis heute.** (Welcome to Berlin: the image of Berlin in the English-speaking world from 1700 until the present.)
      Edited by Jörg Helbig, foreword by Anthony Burgess.   Berlin (West): Stapp, 1987. 192p. bibliog. (Edition Buchexpress).
The emphasis of this volume rests on the twentieth century and on literature. In addition, there are interesting pieces on Berlin as part of the English gentleman's 'Grand Tour' in the eighteenth century, George Eliot's stay in Berlin during the winter of 1854-55, the historian and diplomat George Bancroft in Berlin, Billy Wilder's Berlin films, and the image of Berlin in British and American pop- and rock-songs. Anthony Burgess' short foreword is printed in English and in German translation.

368   **Metropolis: international art exhibition 1991.**
      Edited by Christos M. Joachimides, Norman Rosenthal.   New York: Rizzoli, 1991. 337p. bibliog.
This handsome volume is the catalogue of a successful exhibition held in Berlin in 1991 and devoted to art and the challenges it faces at the beginning of the Nineties: 'We now see before us art in a period of radical change, a kaleidoscope of different artistic approaches, formal positions and differentiated attitudes' (p. 11). The book contains excellent photographs of major exhibits as well as texts by Christos M. Joachimides,

Norman Rosenthal, Wolfgang Max Faust, Achille Bonito Oliva, Christoph Tannert, Boris Groys, Jeffrey Deitch, Jenny Holzer, Vilem Flusser, Dietmar Kamper, and Paul Virilio. There is also a full list of the artists and the works in the exhibition as well as a section (p. 269-320) containing short biographies and notes on the artists.

369 **Die UFA-Story: Geschichte eines Filmkonzerns.** (The UFA story: history of a film concern.)
Klaus Kreimeier. Munich: Hanser, 1992. 520p. bibliog.

Kreimeier's work is a thoroughly researched, detailed and perceptive account of the rise and fall of UFA (Universum-Film AG), the German answer to Hollywood during the Weimar Republic. Founded in Berlin in December 1917 at the instigation of Ludendorff, who saw in it a potential source of uplifting propaganda for his war-weary troops, it was also hijacked by Goebbels for similar purposes in the Second World War, leading in January 1945 to the première of the celebrated Nazi propaganda film *Kolberg.* In spite of this, Kreimeier shows how UFA turned Berlin into a centre of the world film industry with a reputation for producing such classics as *Dr. Mabuse, Metropolis,* and *The Blue Angel.* The volume includes a splendid selection of photographs, an excellent bibliography, and a chronological listing of the main events in UFA's colourful history. This is a useful source of information for anyone with an interest in Berlin's rich cultural tradition. For a discussion of DEFA, the state-subsidized film studio set up by the GDR to take over in the East where UFA had left off in 1945, see *Filmland DDR. Ein Reader zu Geschichte, Funktion und Wirkung der DEFA,* edited by Harry Blunk and Dirk Jungnickel. (Cologne: Verlag Wissenschaft und Politik, 1990. 120p.).

370 **The Berlin Painter.**
Text by Donna Carol Kurtz, drawings by Sir John Beazley. Oxford: Clarendon Press, 1983. 123p. (Oxford Monographs in Classical Archaeology).

The Berlin Painter is a master of Attic red-figured vase-painting who takes his name from a grand amphora in Berlin dating to around 490 BC (reproduced in the book). Fifty-two of the more than 270 vases and fragments attributed to him are featured here and an index contains full information on collections of his work.

371 **100 Jahre Deutsches Theater Berlin 1883-1983.** (A hundred years of the *Deutsches Theater* in Berlin 1883-1983.)
Edited by Michael Kuschnia, introduction by Rolf Rohmer. Berlin, GDR: Henschel, 1983. 517p. bibliog.

This illustrated history of the Deutsches Theater focuses particularly on the eminent directors and actors to whom it largely owes its pre-eminence. The book contains a listing of all the theatre's productions from 1945 to April 1982, including details of productions taken on foreign tours.

372 **Stimme der Kritik I: Berliner Theater 1945-65.** (The voice of criticism: Berlin theatres 1945-1965.)
Friedrich Luft. Frankfurt am Main, FRG; Berlin (West), Vienna: Ullstein, 1982, 526p. (Ullstein Buch Nr. 20180).
Presents a collection of reviews by the acknowledged doyen of post-War Berlin theatre critics.

373 **Berlin and the rise of Modernism 1886-96.**
James McFarlane. In: *Modernism: a guide to European literature 1890-1930.* Edited by Malcolm Bradbury, James McFarlance. Harmondsworth, England: Penguin, 1991, p. 105-19. (Pelican Guides to European Literature).
McFarlane's beautifully written, succinct chapter shows how, for an entire decade, Berlin was a centre of 'intense cultural excitement' (p. 105). The notion of literature as the instrument of social and political progress dominated thinking, with the literary society *Durch* providing a rallying point for young writers. It was in Berlin too that the remarkable upsurge of interest in Ibsen's theatre throughout Europe first took place. Towards the end of the decade the modernists' social preoccupations gave way to an interest in the psychological, and the group's initial unity evaporated in the face of internal dissensions.

374 **Berlinart 1961-1987.**
Edited by Kynaston McShine. Munich: Prestel, 1987. 284p. bibliog.
This book accompanied the exhibition BERLINART 1961-1987, organized by New York's Museum of Modern Art in 1987. In addition to the editor's introduction, it contains six essays (by John Willett, Wieland Schmied, Karl Ruhrberg, René Block, Michael Schwarz, and Laurence Kardish). The volume also contains over 400 photographs, many of them in colour, as well as a chronology of events between 1961 and 1987 (by Thomas Schulte) and biographical details of major artists associated with Berlin (by M. F. Nathanson).

375 **Russen in Berlin: Literatur, Malerei, Theater, Film, 1918-1933.**
(Russians in Berlin: literature, painting, theatre, film, 1918-1933.)
Edited by Fritz Mierau. Leipzig: Reclam, 1990. 2nd ed. 615p. bibliog.
For a decade after the First World War and the Russian Revolution Berlin became, to an extent never matched by any other city outside of Russia, the scene of many of the most significant developments in that country's cultural and intellectual life. It is calculated that there were 300,000 Russians living in Berlin in 1923; a total of about two million passed through the city in the post-War period. So obvious was their presence that the district of Charlottenburg became known to the locals as Charlottengrad, while in 1923 Grieben devoted one of its guides (Nr. 197) to Russian Berlin. Among those who lived in the city at this time were Nabokov, 'the only Russian writer to be produced by Berlin', as Mierau puts it (Nabokov's first seven novels were written and largely take place in Berlin), Pasternak (who rediscovered his voice here in 1922 after a long period of silence), Ehrenburg, Chagall, and Gorki. Augmented by numerous black-and-white photographs, illustrations, and an index, Mierau's judicious selection of documents provides a fascinating overview of the activities of the émigrés, including their interaction with leading German cultural

figures. Also recommended is Robert C. Williams, *Culture in exile. Russian emigrés in Germany 1891-1941* (Ithaca, New York; London: Cornell University Press, 1972).

376 **The city in early cinema: 'Metropolis', 'Berlin' and 'October'.**
Michael Minden. In: *Unreal city: urban experience in modern European literature and art.* Edited by Edward Timms and David Kelley. Manchester, England: Manchester University Press, 1985, p. 193-213. bibliog.

In his sophisticated analysis of the cinematic treatment of the theme of the city in three classical films of the early cinema, Minden offers a challenging interpretation of Walther Ruttmann's *Berlin, die Symphonie der Großstadt* (1927), seeing in it an uneasy tension between a tendency towards abstraction and an interest in social criticism and awareness.

377 **40 Jahre Porzellan: Siegmund Schütz zum 80. Geburtstag.**
(Forty years of porcelain: for Siegmund Schütz on his eightieth birthday.)
Barbara Mundt. Berlin (West): Arenhövel, 1986. 52p. bibliog.

For almost forty years, between 1932 and 1970, Siegmund Schütz was a leading light at the Königliche Porzellan Manufaktur in Berlin, producing for example a number of notable porcelain tea services. This volume contains a full list of his works, some of which are shown in black-and-white photographs. In addition, Barbara Mundt gives a succinct account of the history of porcelain in Berlin and Germany in the twentieth century.

378 **Peter Joseph Lenné.**
Heinz Ohff. Berlin (West): Stapp, 1989. 172p. bibliog. (Preußische Köpfe).

This is an informative study of the achievements of Lenné, the man responsible for designing many of the beautiful parks and gardens which are a feature of the Berlin landscape.

379 **Die Lindenoper: ein Streifzug durch ihre Geschichte.** (The Linden Opera: a survey of its history.)
Werner Otto. Berlin, GDR: Henschel, 1985. 3rd rev. ed. 416p. bibliog.

A readable history of the German State Opera since its founding in 1742. It is popularly known as the Linden Opera because of its location on one of Berlin's most important streets, the Straße Unter den Linden.

380 **The Berlin Secession: Modernism and its enemies in Imperial Germany.**
Peter Paret. Cambridge, Massachusetts; London: Belknap Press of Harvard University Press, 1980. 269p. bibliog.

In the 1890s a wave of protest against the parochialism of much officially approved and promoted art swept across Germany, leading to the formation of numerous separatist movements which became known as 'Secessions'. The birth of the Munich Secession in 1892 was followed by similar developments in Düsseldorf, Dresden, and Weimar, and in 1897 by the Vienna Secession. In his enlightening analysis of the Berlin Secession (founded in 1898), which he regards as an important chapter in official Germany's protracted but ultimately vain attempt to resist Modernism, Paret deals first with the particular situation of the fine arts in Berlin and Germany which gave rise to the Secession and then investigates the most important events which punctuated its controversial existence. These include the conflict over the Secession's wish to participate in the international exposition in Saint Louis (1904) which the United States organized to celebrate the centennial of the Louisiana Purchase. In his carefully documented presentation of the bureaucratic and artistic power struggles which ultimately undermined this wish, Paret sees the whole affair as 'something of a paradigm of the Wilhelmine era' (p. 154). In this and in other affairs, an essentially unfavourable picture emerges of two powerful men representing the forces of tradition; Kaiser Wilhelm II, whose persistent meddling in cultural politics in the name of an imitative, patriotic art did much to provoke the conflict with the Secessionists he was out to suppress, and Anton von Werner, the Secession's most important opponent within the state's two representative organizations for the arts, the Royal Academy of Arts and the Association of Berlin Artists. Paret is able to show that, in striking a blow against Wilhelmine aesthetics and the state's cultural policies, accomplished artists such as Max Liebermann, Walter Leistikow, and Lovis Corinth were able, with the assistance of the gallery owners and publishers Bruno and Paul Cassirer, to turn the Berlin Secession into an 'institutional centre of German Impressionism' which remained 'sufficiently flexible to help pave the way for Expressionism' (p. 1). The volume contains an index and thirteen illustrations.

381 **Die Bauten der Berliner Museumsinsel.** (The buildings on Berlin's museum island.)
Renate Petras, foreword by Günter Schade.   Berlin (West): Stapp, 1987. 227p. bibliog.

The Old Museum, built by Schinkel in 1823-30, was the first museum in Berlin. Over the next hundred years four more museums were built on the 'museum island' which sits in the Spree at the centre of Berlin. This volume looks at the history of how these museums were first constructed and then developed and contains a large selection of historical photographs and plans. Petras lays considerable emphasis on the main personalities involved – the architects, the academics, the sculptors, the painters, and those who provided patronage.

382 **Das gab's nur einmal: die große Zeit des deutschen Films.** (It was unique: the great era of the German cinema.)
Curt Rieß.   Frankfurt am Main, FRG; Berlin (West), Vienna: Ullstein, 1985. 3 vols. (TB 34282-4).

This popular and comprehensive history of UFA (the Universum Film AG, Germany's equivalent of Hollywood) is written in a lively, journalistic style which makes its 900 pages a pleasure to read. Volume one deals with the era of the silent film; volume two with the 'talkies'; and volume three with German film productions up to 1945. Volume three also includes a filmography from all three volumes. Rieß's text is illustrated throughout with numerous photographs. For a classic analysis of many of UFA's best films, see Siegfried Kracauer, *From Caligari to Hitler. A psychological history of the German film.* Princeton, New Jersey: Princeton University Press, 1946. 361p. Kracauer's book, which includes sixty-four black-and-white photographs, argues that these films reveal deep psychological dispositions predominant in Germany from 1918 to 1933.

383   **Heinrich Zille: das graphische Werk.** (Heinrich Zille: the graphic
works.)
Edited by Detlev Rosenbach, with the assistance of Renate Altner,
Matthias Flügge.   Hanover, FRG: Edition Rosenbach, 1984. 228p.
Zille's graphic works are beautifully reproduced in this volume, each accompanied by a
scholarly annotation. For a critical biography of Zille, see Lothar Fischer's *Heinrich
Zille in Selbstzeugnissen und Bilddokumenten* (Heinrich Zille in his own words and in
pictures.) (Reinbek, FRG: Rowohlt, 1979. 157p. bibliog.).

384   **Berlin 1910-1933.**
Eberhard Roters, Janos Frecot, Sonja Günther, Joachim Heusinger
von Waldegg, Ulrich Gregor, Arno Paul, translated from the German
by Marguerite Mounier.   New York: Rizzoli, 1982. 284p. bibliog.
This excellent volume on what Roters in his introduction calls 'Berlin's tremendous
creativity in the years from 1910 to 1930' covers architecture, the fine arts, film, and
theatre, but excludes music and literature. Its five chapters are therefore devoted to
the city architecture and habitat (Janos Frecot, Sonja Günther); painting (Eberhard
Roters); sculpture (Joachim Heusinger von Waldegg); film (Ulrich Gregor); and
theatre (Arno Paul). The volume is illustrated by 296 photographs and includes a
useful guide to persons mentioned in the book (p. 270-76).

385   **Die Berliner Museumsinsel: Zerstörung, Rettung, Wiederaufbau.** (The
Berlin museum island: destruction, rescue, reconstruction.)
Günter Schade.   Berlin, GDR: Henschel, 1986. 160p. bibliog.
Lying at the heart of Berlin is an island on which stand the city's best known museums.
This study covers its history from the destruction wrought by the Nazis to the attempts
at reconstruction made by the GDR up to the mid-1980s. Most of the book (p. 9-126)
is devoted to the period up to 1958, when the Soviet Union returned to the GDR the
works of art which it had removed from Dresden and other centres for safe keeping at
the end of the Second World War. The book also contains numerous illustrations,
some in colour.

386   **Berliner Porzellan: zur Kunst- und Kulturgeschichte der Berliner
Porzellanmanufakturen im 18. und 19. Jahrhundert.** (Berlin porcelain:
on the art history and cultural history of Berlin porcelain manufacture
in the 18th and 19th centuries.)
Günter Schade.   Munich: Keyser, 1987. 228p. bibliog.
In 1751, forty-one years after the establishment in Meißen of the first European centre
for the manufacture of porcelain, Berlin too set up its own production centre. Within a
few years this became one of the leading industries in the city. Günter Schade's history
of porcelain in Berlin, illustrated by 112 photographs, provides a succinct and balanced
introduction to this important aspect of the city's cultural profile.

387 **Damals im Romanischen Café: Künstler und ihre Lokale im Berlin der zwanziger Jahre.** (The Romanisches Café and its times: artists and their cafés in the Berlin of the 1920s.)
Jürgen Schebera. Frankfurt am Main, FRG; Vienna: Büchergilde Gutenberg, 1988. 142p. bibliog.

In the 1920s Berlin's cafés were the favoured meeting-places of many of the city's most prominent writers and artists. Schebera's book introduces the reader to the main figures involved and to the cafés they frequented. An excellent selection of photographs brings alive the atmosphere of the times.

388 **Bertolt Brecht's adaptations for the Berliner Ensemble.**
Arrigo Subiotto. London: Modern Humanities Research Association, 1975. 207p. bibliog.

This is a scholarly investigation of the remarkable adaptations of the classics which Bertolt Brecht produced for his theatre in Berlin, the Berliner Ensemble. Adaptations of plays by Hauptmann, Lenz, Molière, Farquar, and Shakespeare are all examined in detail.

389 **Berlin – Kulturstadt Europas 1988: Cultural City of Europe 1988: Ville Européenne de la culture 1988.**
Edited by Lorenz Tomerius. Frankfurt am Main, FRG; Berlin (West): Ullstein, 1988. 239p.

In 1988 it was West Berlin's turn to follow in the footsteps of cities such as Florence, Athens, and Amsterdam and become Cultural City of Europe for a year. This volume presents the rich programme of events which the various cultural institutions of the city prepared to celebrate the occasion. It includes music, theatre, literature, the fine arts, design, fashion, architecture, and film. In the latter category, Berlin took the major step of initiating a European Film Award, which it was intended should be awarded annually by future Cultural Cities of Europe. The volume includes a foreword by Eberhard Diepgen, the Mayor of Berlin, as well as short essays (with summaries in English and French) by Hans Mayer, Peter Bender, Markus Brüderlin, Heiner Stachelhaus, Axel Hecht, Gerhard R. Koch, Steve Lake, Stephan Stroux, Marcelle Michel, Wolf Donner, and Christian Borngräber. There are also interviews with Nele Hertling, the organizer of a European theatre workshop, and with B. K. Tragelehn on the theatre of Heiner Müller. Numerous photographs intersperse the texts.

390 **Mitte und Grenze: Motive konservativer Kulturpolitik am Beispiel Berlins 1945 bis 1985.** (Centre and border: motifs of conservative cultural policy – the example of Berlin 1945-1985.)
Karin Westermann. Frankfurt am Main, FRG: Peter Lang, 1989. 438p. bibliog. (Europäische Hochschulschriften, Reihe XXXI – Politikwissenschaft, 145).

This work investigates the influence of conservative thinking on cultural policy in West Berlin since the end of the Second World War. It does so by analysing the most important debates and controversies affecting cultural policy in that period. Originally written as a doctoral dissertation, it succeeds in shedding new light on an aspect of Berlin's public life which has not always had the attention it deserves.

391   **The new sobriety 1917-1933: art and politics in the Weimar period.**
John Willett.   London: Thames & Hudson, 1978. 272p. bibliog.

An authoritative analysis of the creative vision often known as the 'New Objectivity'
(Willett prefers to speak of the 'new sobriety') which had its roots in Dada, the
disillusioning experience of the First World War, and the German Revolution of 1918.
Berlin was one of the major centres in which this new vision was articulated and is
therefore a recurring focus in Willett's study, which is admirably comprehensive in
scope and supported by a brilliant selection of photographs. The volume also includes
a 'cultural map of the '20s in mid-Europe', a chronological table, charts, a glossary of
abbreviations, and an index.

392   **The theatre of Erwin Piscator: half a century of politics in the theatre.**
John Willett.   London: Methuen, 1986. 224p. bibliog.

First published in 1978 (London: Eyre Methuen), this knowledgeable and balanced
study was the first book in English to cover the whole of Piscator's career in the
theatre. It includes a comprehensive chronology of the main events, productions, and
publications which punctuated Piscator's colourful life (1893-1966). The book focuses
on Piscator's conception of political theatre and his pursuit of its realization above all
in Berlin, where the first (and commercially unsuccessful) *Piscatorbühne* (literally:
Piscator stage) was opened in 1927. The book contains numerous photographs and a
useful index. Also worth consulting is Maria Ley-Piscator. *The Piscator experiment.*
The political theatre (New York: J. H. Heineman, 1967. 336p.).

Architecture and
Urban Planning

393 **Berliner Wohnungsbaugenossenschaften: eine exemplarische Bestandsaufnahme und analytische Beschreibung der Merkmale des genossenschaftlichen Wohnens in der Gegenwart.** (Berlin building co-operatives: an assessment of some examples, and an analytical description of the characteristics of co-operative living in the present.) Michael Arndt, Holger Rogall. Berlin (West): Berlin Verlag Arno Spitz, 1987. 290p. bibliog. (Berlin Forschung, vol. 16).

Based on the authors' joint doctoral dissertation, this study investigates the main features of Berlin's building co-operatives, their contribution to the development of the city, and the possibility of the further growth of this distinctive aspect of the urban landscape.

394 **Ziel, Begründungen und Methoden des Naturschutzes im Rahmen der Stadtentwicklungspolitik von Berlin.** (Purpose, rationale and methods of nature protection as part of Berlin's policy for civic development.) Axel Auhagen, Herbert Sukopp. *Natur und Landschaft*, no. 58 (1983), p. 9-15.

Blessed with lakes, woodland, and open spaces, Berlin is one of the world's greenest capitals. This informative study deals with the need to ensure that development does not take place at the expense of the city's enviable natural resources.

395 **Berlin: the politics of order: 1737-1989.**
Alan Balfour. New York: Rizzoli, 1990. 269p. bibliog.

Balfour investigates the changing face over 250 years of one small but centrally important area of Berlin – 'a rectangle of land a thousand meters deep and a thousand meters wide on either side of Leipziger Platz, at the heart of the city' (p. 11). The ideas of architects and designers as varied as Gilly, Schinkel, Schmitz, Speer, Mendelsohn, Le Corbusier, Scharoun, Mies van der Rohe, Stirling, Eisenman, and Hollein are discussed competently, if in somewhat flowery language. An abundance of excellent

118

illustrations is a particular strength of this book, which takes as its cut-off point the fall of the Berlin Wall in November 1989.

396 **Bauen in Berlin: 1973 bis 1987.** (Building in Berlin: 1973 to 1983.)
Adalbert Behr, edited by Ehrhardt Gißke, foreword by Ehrhardt
Gißke.   Leipzig, GDR: Koehler & Amelang, 1987. 199p. bibliog.
With around 150 pages of glossy photographs and thirty-four pages of commentary this book celebrates the GDR's efforts since the early 1970s to rebuild East Berlin, particularly its centre,

397 **Synagogen in Berlin: zur Geschichte einer zerstörten Architektur.**
(Synagogues in Berlin: on the history of a destroyed architecture.)
Veronika Bendt, Rolf Bothe, Michael Engel, Harold Hammer-Schenk,
Hans Hirschberg, with the assistance of Antje Gerlach, Raymond
Wolff.   Berlin (West): Arehövel, 1983. 2 vols. bibliog.
(Stadtgeschichtliche Publikationen, vol. 1).
This is the catalogue of an exhibition on Berlin's synagogues which was held at the Berlin Museum from 26 January to 20 March 1983. It contains photographs and diagrams as well as an excellent historical introduction to its theme.

398 **Inside the Bauhaus.**
Howard Dearstyne, edited by David Spaeth.   New York: Rizzoli,
1986. 286p. bibliog.; London: Architectural Press, 1986. 288p. bibliog.
Dearstyne was one of a small number of Americans to study at the Bauhaus and the only one to be awarded a diploma in architecture there. When the Bauhaus closed in Dessau on 1 October 1932 to be opened three weeks later by Mies van der Rohe in Berlin as a private institution without government subsidy, Dearstyne too made the move to the capital. Unfortunately, the experiment was short-lived, and the Nazis closed the school on 11 April 1933. Dearstyne's very personal account of this period relies to a large extent on letters which he wrote at the time. The editor makes very few changes to Dearstyne's manuscript (on which the author had been working at the time of his death in 1979), but he does make one important addition: Mies van der Rohe's description of the closing of the Berlin Bauhaus, which includes his account of a meeting with the Nazi Minister of Culture Alfred Rosenberg (p. 243-45). The book is illustrated with numerous photographs.

399 **Architektur in Berlin 1900-1933.** (Architecture in Berlin 1900-1933.)
Karl-Heinz Hüter.   Stuttgart, Berlin (West): Kohlhammer, 1988.
367p.
This assessment of architecture in Berlin during the first third of the twentieth century includes 520 photographs, of which sixty-two are in colour.

Architecture and Urban Planning

400 **International building exhibition Berlin 1987: examples of a new architecture.**
Edited by Joseph P. Kleihues, Heinrich Klotz, translated from the German by Ian Robson. New York: Rizzoli, 1986. 282p.

This catalogue was produced to accompany the exhibition which took place in the German Museum of Architecture, Frankfurt am Main, as a prelude to the holding of the International Building Exhibition itself in Berlin in 1987. The drawings presented in the catalogue relate not only to those projects which were actually carried out in Berlin but also to others which did not progress beyond the drawing-board. Also available is *International Building Exhibition 1987* (Tokyo: [n.p.] 1987. 302p.), a generously-illustrated volume which offers a comprehensive overview of the major projects presented at the exhibition. The text is in English and Japanese.

401 **Der Berliner Dom: Bauten, Ideen und Projekte vom 15. Jahrhundert bis zur Gegenwart.** (Berlin Cathedral: buildings, ideas and projects from the fifteenth century to the present.)
Karl-Heinz Klingenburg. Berlin (East): Union Verlag, 1987. 296p. bibliog.

Klingenburg's book is a beautifully illustrated study of Berlin Cathedral's colourful history across five centuries, as seen from the perspective of a GDR specialist.

402 **Architecture and politics in Germany, 1918-1945.**
Barbara Miller Lane. Cambridge, Massachusetts; London: Harvard University Press, 1985. 2nd ed. 278p. bibliog.

This excellent study comments perceptively on the more than 14,000 dwelling units which were built by radical architects in Berlin between 1924 and 1933, notably the 'horseshoe' development in Berlin-Brietz, the 'forest' development in Berlin-Zehlendorf, and the 'Siemensstadt' quarter of the city. She points out, however, that it was not the city administration which was the moving force behind these projects but building societies such as the 'Gehag' (Gemeinnützige Heimstätten-Aktiengesellschaft), of which the guiding spirit was Martin Wagner.

403 **Berlin morgen: Ideen für das Herz einer Großstadt.** (Berlin tomorrow: ideas for the heart of a metropolis.)
Edited by Vittorio Magnago, Michael Mönninger with the assistance of Volker Fischer, Anna Meseure. Stuttgart: Verlag Gerd Hatje, 1991. 174p. bibliog.

The catalogue of an exhibition of the same title which took place in Frankfurt am Main in January-March 1991 before moving to Berlin. It presents the ideas of twenty of the world's most renowned architects for the rebuilding of Berlin's historic centre following the fall of the Wall and the reconstitution of Berlin as a single unified city. The volume also includes sixteen essays by various authors on important aspects of Berlin, all of which had previously appeared as part of a series published by the *Frankfurter Allgemeine Zeitung*. Of particular interest is the call by Joachim Fest for the reconstruction of the famous palace of the Hohenzollerns, reduced to a ruin in the Second World War and razed to the ground in the early 1950s in order to make room for the GDR's Palace of the Republic (p. 76-79). The volume is superbly illustrated.

404   **Die große Zerstörung Berlins: zweihundert Jahre Stadtbaugeschichte.**
(The great destruction of Berlin: two hundred years of municipal
architecture.)
Hans Reuther.   Berlin (West): Propyläen, 1985. 210p. bibliog.

In seven chronologically-ordered sections the author describes what he sees as the
disastrous history of urban development in Berlin from the death of Frederick the
Great (1786) to the mid-1980s.

405   **Architecture in progress: internationale Bauausstellung Berlin 1984.**
Edited by Frank Russell.   London: Architectural Design, 1983. 128p.
(Architectural Design Profile.)

Berlin's International Architecture Competition (IBA) of 1984 was an ambitious
project aimed at rebuilding four areas of West Berlin: Prager Platz; Tegel; southern
Tiergarten; and southern Friedrichstadt. This publication presents an interim account
of the open and invited competitions associated with the project. Copiously illustrated,
it includes articles by Doug Clelland, Joseph Paul Kleihues, Vittorio Magnago
Lampugnani, and Wolfgang Braunfels as well as full details of the competitions. It
closes with a critical article by Colin Rowe on the IBA's proposals: 'IBA is being
expected to do too much with too little'.

406   **Germany in transition: new strategies of urban development.**
Judith Ryser, preface by Elmar Brandt.   London: City State
Publishing, 1991. 72p.

Based on the findings of an Anglo-German seminar held at the Goethe Institute in
London in January 1991, this booklet discusses issues facing urban planners in a city
such as Berlin following the revolutionary upheavals of 1989.

407   **Metropolis Berlin? Prospects and problems of post-November 1989
urban developments.**
Fritz Schmoll.   *International Journal of Urban and Regional Research*,
vol. 14, no. 4 (1990), p. 676-86.

Writing in May/June 1990, Schmoll predicts that the unfication of Germany will have a
major effect on urban development in and around Berlin, attracting substantial
investment (at the expense of other parts of the former GDR) but also causing harmful
social polarization between the employed and the rising number of unemployed. He
foresees a rapid process of suburbanization as the city's population grows, with the
danger that the local population will increasingly be displaced as a result of rising land
values and living costs. He warns against the likelihood that this will lead to the
appearance of ghettoes for those who have been marginalized by the city's
transformation and advocates careful political monitoring and control of social and
spatial developments as well as increased state investment in infrastructure, urban
renewal, and public service quality.

408   **Metropolis 1890-1940.**
Edited by Anthony Sutcliffe.   London: Mansell, 1984. 458p. bibliog.
(Studies in History, Planning, and the Environment).

This is a collection of sixteen scholarly essays on what the editor calls 'the giant city
phenomenon'. Of particular relevance to Berlin are Theda Shapiro's 'The metropolis

in the visual arts: Paris, Berlin, New York 1890-1940' and Horst Matzerath's 'Berlin, 1890-1940'. The book also includes numerous photographs and figures.

409 **Hohnzollern Berlin: construction and reconstruction.**
Robert R. Taylor.   Port Credit, Ontario, Canada: P. D. Meany, 1985.
227p. bibliog. map.

Taylor sets out both to recount the history of Berlin's built environment and also to consider the debate over the restoration of its royal architecture which began in 1945 and continues with new fervour today. The Royal Palace, the Brandenburg Gate, the Emperor William Monument, the Reichstag and the City Hall are among the outstanding artefacts selected for particular attention. The book includes fifty-seven photographs and maps.

410 **Das Neue Berlin: Großstadtprobleme.** (The new Berlin: the problems of a metropolis.)
Edited by Martin Wagner, Adolf Behne, foreword by Julius Posener.
Basel, Switzerland; Berlin (West); Boston, Massachussetts: Birkhäuser, 1988. 268p. bibliog.

The journal *Das Neue Berlin* was founded in 1929 and ran to only twelve issues before it became a victim of Black Friday and the beginning of the world economic crisis. Despite its short life it became an important focus for the ideas of modern architects and city planners such as Bruno Taut, Walter Gropius, and Marcel Breuer. In their foreword to the first issue Martin Wagner and Adolf Behne said of their vision of the metropolis they wished to see grow up in Berlin: 'Let it be our task to collect all works, ideas and achievements which can contribute to making Berlin a place of happy work and happy leisure'. They foresaw a transformation of the city in the following twenty years, in particular through the provision of new suburban housing and the need to accommodate the growth of traffic in the centre. Beautifully illustrated, this reprint of an important journal (first published by Deutsche Bauzeitung in Berlin in 1929) gives a clear impression of the Berlin that might have developed but for the rise of the Third Reich.

411 **German architecture and the classical ideal 1740-1840.**
David Watkin, Tilman Mellinghoff.   London: Thames & Hudson, 1987. 296p. bibliog.

The authors of this study devote an informative chapter to the architect Schinkel (p. 85-117) and another to the Franco-Prussian school and the 'style for a nation' of which Schinkel was such a prominent exponent (p. 59-84). The book is well illustrated.

412 **Erich Mendelsohn.**
Bruno Zevi.   London: Architectural Press; New York: Rizzoli, 1985. 206p. bibliog.

Zevi's assessment of Erich Mendelsohn's stature as an architect includes a chapter devoted to the 'expressionist functionalism' of his work in Berlin (p. 54-127). This is illustrated by a number of excellent black-and-white photographs of the major buildings which Mendelsohn designed for the German capital.

The Media

Mass Media

413 **Medienstadt Berlin.** (Media city Berlin.)
Edited by Günter Bentele, Otfried Jaren. Berlin (West): Vistas, 1988.
638p. bibliog.
Written by a variety of authors, this comprehensive overview deals with a mix of
topics: the history of the media; the press; portraits of individual newspapers; the
radio; the media in East Berlin; future perspectives; cinema; video; books and
publishers; theatre; music; museums; libraries; and the training of journalists. Also
included is a list of important media addresses.

414 **Zeitungsstadt Berlin: Menschen und Mächte in der Geschichte der
deutschen Presse.** (Newspaper city Berlin: people and power in the
history of the German press.)
Peter de Mendelssohn. Berlin (West): Ullstein, 1960. 523p. bibliog.
Describing itself as an 'attempt to write a biography', de Mendelssohn's study presents
a comprehensive picture of Berlin as a centre of the newspaper industry.

415 **The rise and fall of the house of Ullstein.**
Hermann Ullstein. London: Nicolson & Watson, [n.d. 1944?] 256p.
This is a fascinating and highly readable account of the history of the Ullstein
publishing house. Dating back to 1877 when Leopold Ullstein bought the *Berliner
Zeitung*, it became the greatest enterprise of its kind in the world. The fact that it was
owned by Jews made it anathema to the Nazis, who, when they assumed power in
1933, rapidly took over the enterprise and turned it to their own purposes. The story is
told by Hermann Ullstein, Leopold's son by his second wife.

Newspapers and magazines

416   **Berliner Morgenpost. Berliner Allgemeine. Zeitung der deutschen Hauptstadt. Unabhängig.** (Berlin Morning Post. Berlin General. Newspaper of the German capital. Independent.)
Berlin: Axel Springer Verlag. 1898- .

Founded in 1898, the *Morgenpost* is part of the newspaper empire built up in post-War Germany by Axel Springer. It adopts a basically middle-brow approach, avoiding both the sensationalist excesses of the 'yellow' press and the intellectual weightiness characteristic of 'serious' German newspapers.

417   **B. Z.** (*Berliner Zeitung*). (B. Z. [Berlin Newspaper].)
Berlin: Axel Springer Verlag. 1897- .

B. Z. is Berlin's own tabloid newspaper. Like *Morgenpost*, it was part of the newspaper empire constructed by arguably Germany's most important post-War media mogul, Axel Springer. Gossip, scandal, and topical human interest stories feature prominently in its pages.

418   **Bild. Unabhängig. Überparteilich.** (Picture. Independent. Above party.)
Berlin: Axel Springer Verlag. 1952- .

Like *B. Z.* (*Berliner Zeitung*) this is a tabloid from the Springer publishing house. It is a truly national newspaper, however, with its headquarters in Hamburg. A special Berlin edition is published which reflects the local concerns of the capital. *Bild* is the most widely read newspaper in Germany and, at only 60 *pfennigs* a copy, one of the cheapest.

419   **die tageszeitung.** (the daily paper.)
Berlin: Freunde der Alternativen Tageszeitung. 1978- .

Usually known by its abbrieviated title as *taz*, this left-wing newspaper is the youngest of Berlin's major papers and is widely respected for the intelligence of its reporting. However, it relies for its survival on the idealism of its staff, who work for considerably less financial reward than journalists on other newspapers. Whether this will ensure its continued publication over the coming years remains to be seen.

420   **tip. Berlin Magazin.** (tip. Berlin Magazine.)
Edited by Klaus Stemmler.   Berlin: TIP Verlag.

tip appears every second Wednesday in Berlin and one day later in other parts of Germany. Each issue contains full information of cultural events in Berlin over the following two weeks as well as details of television and radio programmes for the same period. Like its rival, *Zitty* (the two publications appear in alternate weeks), *tip* also offers a variety of feature articles, reviews and interviews in a typical issue, which will contain approximately 300 pages.

421   **Zitty. Illustrierte Stadtzeitung Berlin.** (Zitty. Illustrated city newspaper
      Berlin.)

Zitty is a comprehensive source of information for any visitor to Berlin who wants to
know what's happening in the city's rich cultural life. It appears every second
Wednesday and contains a variety of articles and reviews, readers' letters, small ads.,
useful addresses, details of television and radio programmes as well as of current
events in Berlin (theatre, cinema, lectures etc.). It shares these features with its
immediate rival, *tip. Berlin Magazin*, which also appears every second Wednesday but
during the weeks when *Zitty* is not for sale.

Bibliographies

422 **Kiepert Berlin-Literatur Verzeichnis zur 750-Jahr-Feier 1987: eine Bibliographie lieferbarer Bücher und Karten.** (Kiepert's listing of literature on Berlin, to mark Berlin's 750th anniversary: a bibliography of books and maps in print.)
Edited by Berlin-Abteilung der Buchhandlung Kiepert. Berlin (West): Kiepert, 1986. 9th rev. ed. 290p.

Kiepert, one of Berlin's leading bookshops, regularly produces an up-dated edition of its bibliography of publications on Berlin. The ninth edition reflects the enormous interest aroused in all matters relating to Berlin by the city's 750th anniversary in 1987, containing nearly 1400 entries, an index, and ten photographs; a further revision of this edition in 1987 saw the number of entries swell to 1640; in 1988 a supplement was published as the tenth edition, this containing a further 410 titles. Readers with a good knowledge of German are referred to this excellent source of regularly updated information on German books in print on Berlin (available from Buchhandlung Kiepert, Hardenbergstraße 4-5, D-1000 Berlin 12. Tel. Berlin 31 10 09-0).

423 **Willy Brandt: Personalbibliographie.** (Willy Brandt: bibliography of his writings.)
Compiled by Ruth Großgart, Hermann Rösch-Sondermann, Rüdiger Zimmermann, Horst Ziska, foreword by Holger Börner. Bonn; Bad Godesberg, Germany: Friedrich Ebert Stiftung, 1990. 410p. (Bibliothek der sozialen Demokratie/ Bibliothek der Friedrich Ebert Stiftung).

This bibliography of Willy Brandt's writings and speeches was produced to mark his seventy-fifth birthday in 1990. Except for the pre-War period it disclaims any pretence to completeness, particularly as regards the many texts by Brandt which appeared anonymously or in translation. Nevertheless, it lists almost 3,500 titles.

424 **Zeitschriften-Bibliographie zur Architektur in Berlin von 1919 bis 1945.**
(Bibliography of periodicals articles on architecture in Berlin from 1919
to 1945.)
Peter Güttler, Sabine Güttler. Berlin (West): Mann, 1986. 723p.
bibliog. (Die Bauwerke und Kunstdenkmäler von Berlin, Beiheft 14).
This comprehensive bibliography of articles on the architecture of Berlin between 1919
and 1945 covers 133 journals and 12,000 references and includes six indexes.

425 **Berlin 750 years: a selective bibliography.**
Margrit B. Krewson. Washington, DC: Library of Congress, 1986.
62p.
This useful short bibliography was produced by a specialist librarian at the Library of
Congress to mark the 750th anniversary of Berlin's founding. It includes an index.

426 **Berlin-Bibliogaphie (1978 bis 1984).** (Berlin bibliography [1978 to
1984].)
Ute Schäfer, Rainald Stromeyer, with the assistance of Renate Korb,
Dorothea Reinhold, Ursula Scholz, Frances Toma, foreword by Klaus
Zernack, Rainald Stromeyer. Berlin (West), New York: de Gruyter,
1987. 1,121p. (Veröffentlichungen der Historischen Kommission zu
Berlin, vol. 69: Bibliographies, vol. 6).
This volume is an indispensable tool for any researcher on Berlin. Its ambitious aim is
to provide a bibliography which reflects Berlin in all its aspects, in the present and in
the past, whether seen from the outside or from within. It contains 13,000 references,
arranged under nine headings, and is comprehensively indexed. It is the fourth in a
series of bibliographies, the others being: *Berlin-Bibliographie (bis 1960)* by Hans
Zopf, Gerd Heinrich; *Berlin-Bibliographie (1961 bis 1966)*, by Ursula Scholz, Rainald
Stromeyer, with the assistance of Edith Scholz; *Berlin-Bibliographie (1967 bis 1977)*,
by Ursula Scholz, Rainald Stromeyer, with the assistance of Renate Korb, Frances
Toma. All were published in West Berlin and New York by de Gruyter in 1965, 1973
and 1984 respectively. A fifth volume, covering 1985-1990, is planned for the early
1990s. Subsequent volumes should appear at five-year intervals.

427 **Veröffentlichungen des statistischen Landesamtes Berlin seit 1945.**
(Publications of the Statistical Office of the Land of Berlin since 1945.)
Berlin: Statistisches Landesamt Berlin, 1991. 52p.
This useful bibliography, which is up-dated annually, lists all the publications of the
Statistical Office of the Land of Berlin since 1945. These are grouped under twenty-
three headings, for example health, elections, public finances, prices, and environmen-
tal protection. They are available from: Kulturbuch-Verlag, Sproßerweg 3, 1000 Berlin
47 (Tel. Berlin 661 84 84).

428 **Architecture of Berlin : recent journal articles.**
Mary Vance. Monticello, Illinois: Vance Bibliographies, 1987. 26p.
Presents a useful listing of articles on Berlin's architecture.

429 **Berlin: eine Bibliographie: systematischer Katalog lieferbarer Berlin-Bücher und -Karten.** (Berlin. A bibliography: systematic catalogue of books and maps in print on Berlin.)
   Edited by Daniel Widmaier.   Berlin (West): Elwert & Meurer, 1987.

A comprehensive bibliography of books and maps available through booksellers such as Elwert & Meurer.

Indexes

There follow three separate indexes: authors (personal and corporate); titles; and subjects. Title entries are italicized and refer either to the main titles, or to other works cited in the main titles, or to other works cited in the annotations. The numbers refer to bibliographic entries, not to pages. Individual index entries are arranged in alphabetical sequence.

Index of Authors

K

Kaak, H. 32
Kästner, Erich 346, 347
Kamke, H. U. 32
Kampen, W. van 323
Kamper, D. 368
Kane, M. 117
Kardish, L. 374
Karner, S. 142
Kass, S. 69
Katzur, K. 33
Kaye, M. M. 348
Keegan, J. 130
Keiderling, G. 225
Kelch, J. 76, 77
Keller, F. E. 21
Kelley, D. 376
Kemp, A. 263
Kemper, G. H. 219
Kerndl, A. 138
Kerr, J. 349
Kerstan, R. 194
Kiaulehn, W. 157
Kiersch, G. 195
King, L. J. 350
Kirchhoff, G. 2
Kisker, K. P. 316
Klaus, R. 195
Kleihues, J. P. 400, 405
Klein, D. 287
Kleinschmidt, H. G. 146
Kliem, P. G. 320
Klingenburg, K. H. 401
Klös, H. G. 85
Kloos, R. 304
Klotz, H. 400
Klünner, H. W. 17, 21
Knobloch, H. 33
Koch, G. R. 389
Koch, H. W. 156, 160
Koch, T. 56
Köhler, G. 141
Köhler, W. H. 76, 77
Kohlschütter, K. 53
Kohte, J. 14
Koptelzew, W. 226
Korb, R. 426
Kracauer, S. 382
Krafft, H. 7, 19
Kramer, W. 195
Kramp, H. 316
Kreimeier, K. 369
Krell, M. 118

Krewson, M. B. 425
Kriecken, R. van 63
Krieger, P. 82
Krier, L. 126
Krum, H. 3
Kruse, M. 3
Kuby, E. 196
Kuehn, H. R. 188
Kurella, A. 197
Kurschat, H. 14
Kurthen, H. 303
Kurtz, D. C. 370
Kuschnia, M. 371
Kuzdas, H. J. 264

L

Laabs, R. 86
Lake, S. 389
Lampugnani, V. M. 405
Lane, B. M. 402
Lange, A. 172
Langguth, G. 226
Laqueur, W. 173
Lawler, E. 327
Lehnartz, D. 26
Lehnartz, K. 26
Lemke, U. 324
Lengefeld, L. 12
Lewis, B. I. 117
Levy, L. 7
Ley-Piscator, M. 392
Liang, H. H. 174, 227
Liebmann, I. 31
Liedtke, K. 26
Lips, E. 200
List, F. K. 39
Litten, I. 198
Livingstone, R. 346
Löwenthal, R. 122, 240
Loock, H. D. 104
Luft, F. 372
Lynch, P. 18

M

McAdams, J. A. 291
McEwan, I. 351
McClelland, C. E. 25, 266
McCloy, J. J. 214

McFarlane, J. 373
MacPhedran, G. 57
McShine, K. 374
Maaß, W. 20
Magdelaine, M. 3
Magnago, V. 403
Mahncke, D. 267, 285
Mandell, R. D. 180
Mander, J. 143, 265
Manheim, R. 242
Manvell, R. 130
Marabini, J. 199
Marcus, P. E. 118
Mare, W. de la 347
Martin, D. C. 351
Martin, E. 125
Martiny, A. 78
Mastny, V. 272
Masur, G. 157
Matzerath, H. 312, 408
Mayer, H. 389
Medlicott, W. N. 158
Melcher, P. 4
Mellinghoff, T. 411
Melzer, R. 87
Mendelssohn, P. de 414
Menzel, M. 93
Merritt, A. J. 267
Merritt, R. L. 220, 267
Meseure, A. 403
Metcalfe, P. 200
Metzger, K. H. 88
Meyer, M. 292
Miall, B. 198
Michalowski, B. 26
Michel, M. 389
Middlebrook, M. 201
Mierau, F. 375
Miller, J. 257
Minden, M. 376
Mintzel, A. 219
Missmann, M. 17
Mönninger, M. 403
Mohr, H. 245
Mommsen, W. J. 153
Momper, W. 26, 264
Morris, E. 237
Morris, S. 341
Mounier, M. 384
Mouton, J. C. 64
Müller, H. H. 354
Mundt, B. 377
Mussey, B. 184

Index of Titles

138

Index of Subjects

see also individual
districts by name e.g.
Spandau, Steglitz,
Wedding
Doenitz, Karl (war
criminal) 110
Döblin, Alfred (writer)
165, 340, 342
Dr. Mabuse (film) 369
Dodd, Martha (daughter
of US Ambassador)
200
Dodd, William (US
Ambassador) 200
Dresden 385
secession art movement
380
Drexel, Constance (radio
traitor) 181
Dronke, Ernst 159
Drug abuse 223, 301, 305
see also Society
Duncan, Isadora 115
Durch (literary group) 373
Düsseldorf
secession art movement
380

E

Eagle (symbol of Prussia)
143
Economy 9, 62
Berlinzulage (additional
payment) 314
corporation tax 314
East Berlin
development 311, 313,
317
structure 311
tertiary sector 311
income tax 170, 314
overview 315
post-Reunification
economy 292, 314
post-Wall economic
viability 265
post-War 19, 219, 223,
226, 241, 267, 316
prices 427

problems 312
public finance 427
reparations 310
statistics 333
tax privileges 314
VAT 170
West Berlin
structure 311
tertiary sector 311
women in the workplace
317
see also History
Education 62, 128, 254
Berlin as centre of
research 223
East German 317
history curriculum 330
schools 223
teaching of science and
technology 325, 329
see also Science
EEC see European
Economic Community
Egyptian Museum 80
Ehrenburg, Ilya (writer)
375
Einstein, Albert 177
Eisenhower, Dwight D.
204
Eisenman, Peter
(architect) 395
Elbe (river) 135
Eliot, George (writer) 367
Emperor William
Monument 409
Employment
foreign labour 303
gender and employment
303
labour market 303
unemployment 223
Engels, Friedrich 159
see also Politics
Engravings 3
Environmental protection
427
Erbe, Michael 138
Escapes
from East Berlin 5, 127,
221, 249, 256-257, 263,
267-268, 272, 274, 357
from Nazi Germany 206
from West Berlin 221

Espionage 193
agents provocateurs 243
Europa-Center 320
Europe
Berlin's role in 226, 293
GDR role 237
Europe, Eastern 303
collapse of 105, 226, 243,
248
post-War 216, 228
European Economic
Community (EEC)
286, 293
Expressionism 380

F

Fallada, Hans (author) 342
Farquar, George
(playwright) 388
Fashion 389
Fassbinder, Rainer Werner
(film director) 340
Faust, Wolfgang Max
(artist) 368
Fechter, Peter (killed
whilst crossing the
Wall) 274
Federal Republic 213
Films 81, 109, 180, 263,
301, 338, 340, 345,
366-367, 369, 376, 382,
384, 389, 413
Fire service 79
Flora and fauna 28, 85, 92,
394
moss 93-94
Flusser, Vilem (artist) 368
Fontane, Theodor 137,
162, 341-342, 356
Food
supplies during Berlin
Blockade 239
see also Cuisine
Foreign migrants 223,
295-296, 303
Foreign policy
West German 291
Foreign relations 149, 153,
158, 230
Anglo-German 96, 150,
192

150

155

W

Wagner, Martin (architect) 402, 410
Walker, Ian (journalist) 132
Walking 46, 52, 60, 68
Wall, Berlin *see* Berlin Wall
Wandervogel youth movement 141, 167
War criminals *see* individual by name e.g. Speer, Albert
Wars of Liberation (1813-15) 331
Warsaw 248
Warsaw Pact 226
Water towers 142
Weavers uprising 159
  see also Industrial relations
Wedding (district) 32
Wegscheider, Dr. (Weimar head of education) 103
Wehrmacht 205
Weisäcker, Richard von (former Mayor of Berlin) 226

Weißensee (district) 4, 33
Werner, Anton von (opponent of the Berlin Secession) 380
Wessels, Horst (Nazi martyr) 186
Wigman, Mary (dancer) 115
Wilder, Billy 118, 347, 367
Wilhelm II, Kaiser 112, 172, 380
Wilhelmstraße 74
Wilmersdorf (district) 32
Wirsing, Sybille 138
Wittenbergplatz 320
Wolff, Marion Freyer (Jewish Berliner) 133
Wolff, Theodor (newspaper editor) 115
Women 141, 212
  emancipation 155
  Jewish 155
  work 303
Working class 154, 175, 353
  see also History (Workers' Uprising)

Wozzeck 165

Y

Youth 167
  post-Hitler 255
  see also individual youth groups e.g. Hitlerjugend, Wandervogel

Z

Zaisser, Wilhelm (member of SED) 246
ZDF (Zweites Deutsches Fernsehen) 271
Zehlendorf (district) 32
  housing development 402
Zeller, Frederic (writer) 134
Zille, Heinrich (artist) 23, 383
Zitty 420-421
Zoo station 132, 320

Map of Berlin

This map shows the more important towns and other features.

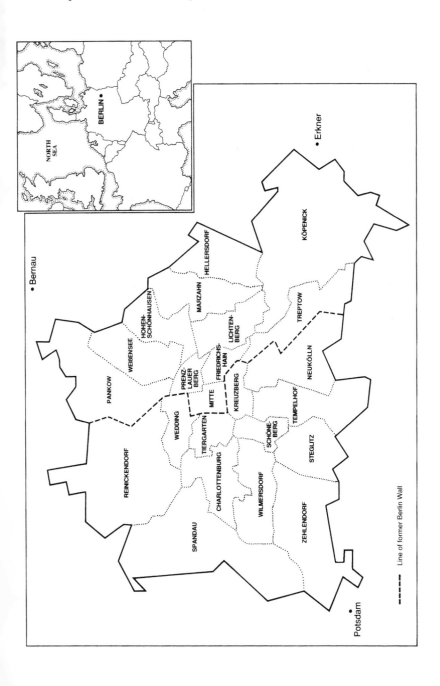